BUILDING POSITIVE MINDSET FOR WEALTH

The mindset of a wealth Person
Mastering your Thoughts for Financial
Freedom
Understanding the law of attraction

By

Milton E. Morgan

TABLE OF CONTENTS

INTRODUCTION

We all celebrate successes, fawning over the accomplishments of others. Yet we seldom admit that failures frequently prepare the route to success. With our concentration focused on bright achievements, we seek success but dread the process that will lead us there. It's absurd to expect to triumph without ever experiencing defeat. Consider these remarkable "successful failures";

One of the most recognized television presenters and the world's first black billionaire, was sacked from her post as a TV anchor in Baltimore. The producer concluded she was not qualified to be on screen.

Walt Disney, one of the most recommended animators, was sacked from one of his first jobs at the Kansas City Star because the editor felt he "lacked the ability to create and had no excellent ideas."

King of horror Stephen King almost gave up his goal of writing when Carrie was rejected by 30 publishers. King dumped the book in the garbage, but his wife fished it out and encouraged him to try again. Not long after, Carrie was released, and King went down in history as one of the greatest horror novelists of our time.

So, how did their failures finally feed their success? It boils down to mentality. Stanford University psychologist Carol Dweck is notable for her study on mentality and its role in motivation, self-regulation, and achievement. She differentiates growing and fixed mindsets, observing how the two viewpoints affect how we confront setbacks. But before we dig into development and fixed mindsets, let's be on the same page on what we mean by "mindset."

Defining "mindset"

Mindset is a collection of strongly held, powerful ideas that impact your vision of yourself and the world around you. A framework for work and life, it's the lens through which you evaluate possibilities and your capacity to solve problems. Mindset has a crucial impact in your connection with success and failure.

After thirty years, studies has revealed that the vision you select for yourself substantially influences the way you run your life. It may decide whether you become the person you want to be and if you achieve the things you value.

Carol Dweck, Stanford University Psychologist and author of Mindset: The New Psychology of Success.

What can we say about growth and fixed mentality?

A fixed mentality is the notion that your abilities, skills, and intellect are intrinsic and unchangeable. Regardless of your effort, you have little impact on them. In this manner, the hand you are dealt in life influences what you may accomplish.

A growth mindset is the concept that your abilities, skills, and intellect are changeable and can be developed through time, practice, and effort. It acknowledges that although everyone has diverse aptitudes and interests, we all have the ability to progress.

Relationship between Success and Failure

Growth and fixed mindsets perceive success and failure quite differently depending on their set of ideas.

Fixed Mentality

Success: For someone with a fixed mentality, the assumption that talents are innate and unchangeable increases pressure to "prove" oneself. Those with a fixed mentality spend their energy on methods to show they are "better" than others.

Failure: Operating out of insecurity, someone with a fixed attitude responds competitively and defensively in an attempt to confirm their "natural" qualities. Failure is a peril they must guard themselves against. Mistakes disclose vulnerabilities and weaknesses are signs of human inadequacy. Those with a fixed attitude don't learn from their errors, dismissing criticism and passing responsibility onto their environment. In a fixed perspective, failure sounds like; "Failure is the limit of my abilities."

"I can either do it or I can't."

"I give up when I'm frustrated."

This attitude prevents advancement by strong fear of failure, protecting the individual from difficulties that may lead to growth.

Growth Mentality

Success: In a growth mentality, success is secondary to development. Rather than concentrating on outcomes, someone with a development mindset enjoys the work they put in and appreciates the milestones along the route. They know that hard work and devotion lead to learning and progress - success is only a result of their efforts. Fueled by personal motivation, someone with a development mentality isn't bothered about others' acceptance.

Failure: For someone with a growth mentality, failure isn't a fault – it's a learning opportunity. Making errors is part of a process of discovery, enabling people to enhance their knowledge. Those with growth mindsets accept responsibility for their blunders and move on, realizing that they are not failing if they're learning. This mentality makes people more inclined to attempt new things since curiosity pulls them onward. Constructive criticism and input are encouraged as important assets.

Steps to Create a Growth Mindset

A growth mindset is beneficial to success because it helps you to venture out of your comfort zone, learn from your errors, and stay resilient in the face of setbacks. Cultivating a growth mindset requires intention, but over time you'll enjoy the advantages of more drive, accomplishment, and delight.

There are a few ways you might begin tapping into and creating a development mindset:

Identify where you have a stuck thinking

Your mentality isn't static; you probably have a development mindset in some areas and a fixed mindset in others. To determine where you have a stuck attitude, pay attention to where you prefer to avoid or discontinue what you know is healthy for you. Feelings of boredom, worry, and discomfort might also signify areas you see as unchangeable.

Seek input

Recognize that others can help make you better-after all, it's impossible to think you can perfect all aspects of your job and life. Constructive criticism is a wonderful tool that helps you to detect blind spots, so don't be scared to ask people where you might improve.

Embrace failure

You are going to make errors, and that's alright. Take responsibility for your blunders. When you blame your circumstances or shift responsibility, you deny yourself the ability to change it. After a mistake, become intrigued. Ask yourself, "What obstacles kept me from achieving my goal?"

Pursue challenges

Taking on initiatives that expand your abilities is a chance to improve that prepares you for better opportunities in the future. Don't pass up possibilities because you don't feel as if you have a good grip on the abilities necessary. Reframe how you think about obstacles think of them as an opportunity, experiment, or adventure.

Ask questions. Take use of others' knowledge by asking questions. After all, no one knows everything. Rather of being afraid or humiliated about your lack of information, become intrigued! If you're terrified of seeming ignorant, remember that the criticism you fear from others isn't as severe as your own inner critic.

Take pride in the journey

Focus on your development, not outcomes. When you obsess on the final objective, you lose sight of the lessons you may gain along the road. The aim is to learn and develop, not succeed.

Praise effort, not talents

When you focus on your present talents, you're thinking about them in a static manner. Instead, take pleasure in your hard work and appreciate your ever-increasing ability to learn and create new talents.

Use the power of "yet"

Are you struggling to accomplish a goal or execute a task? Remind yourself you haven't perfected it "yet." Reframing the difficulty by utilizing "yet" offers open potential and reminds you that you can still go ahead despite setbacks.

Understanding the Wealth Mindset

The notion of a "wealth mindset" goes beyond merely collecting riches; it involves a set of attitudes, beliefs, and actions that may completely impact your relationship with money and financial success.

1. Redefining Wealth

The first step in acquiring a wealth mentality is to redefine wealth itself. It's not only about large quantities of money; it's about plenty in all aspects of life. This involves financial success, but also incorporates health, relationships, personal development, and a feeling of purpose. By widening the notion of wealth, you open yourself up to a better and more rewarding existence.

2. Shifting from Scarcity to Abundance

A wealth mentality entails transitioning from a scarcity perspective, which focuses on restrictions and lack, to an abundance mindset, which sees chances and possibilities everywhere. We'll cover the major distinctions between these two attitudes and how to make the adjustment.

3. Beliefs and Self-Talk

Your attitudes about money and achievement play a key influence in your financial path. We'll identify common limiting ideas and how to confront and replace them with empowering attitudes that support your wealth-building activities. Additionally, we'll cover the impact of positive self-talk and how it may promote a wealth mentality.

4. The Law of Attraction

The law of attraction implies that like attracts like. When you have a good mentality and picture your financial objectives, you may bring riches and opportunity into your life. We'll investigate the physics and ideas underlying the law of attraction and present practical exercises to harness its power.

5. Goal Setting and Clarity
A wealth mentality is founded on clear financial objectives. We'll walk you through the process of defining SMART (Specific, Measurable, Achievable, Relevant, Time-bound) goals and the necessity of keeping focus and clarity on your objectives.

6. Embracing Risk and Learning from Failure
Successful wealth builders recognize that taking appropriate risks is crucial. We'll cover how to handle and accept risk as a development opportunity, as well as the value of learning from financial setbacks and mistakes.

7. Gratitude and Giving Back
Appreciating what you have and practicing appreciation may generate additional riches.

We'll discuss the link between thankfulness and riches, as well as the joy that comes from giving back to people and donating to organizations you're passionate about.

8. Developing Financial Literacy

A wealth mentality is also influenced by financial understanding. We'll touch upon the relevance of financial literacy and continual learning, arming you with the skills required to make educated financial choices.

MORE ON UNDERSTANDING THE WEALTH MINDSET

Understanding the wealth mindset is the basis upon which your route to financial success is constructed. By adopting these concepts and practices, you'll be better able to negotiate the world of money, open doors to possibilities, and begin on a road toward financial plenty.

In the grand tapestry of life, many aspire to achieve financial success - a journey that requires not only astute financial planning but also a transformative change in mindset. The concept of the *"wealth mindset"* is not merely about accumulating wealth but rather about fostering a set of beliefs, attitudes, and behaviors that pave the way for prosperity. It's a way of thinking and living that holds the keys to financial achievement. In this essay, we will delve into the principles and practices that constitute the wealth mindset, revealing how it can guide individuals on their path to financial abundance.

Vision and Clarity

At the core of the wealth mindset lies a vivid and unwavering vision of financial goals. This vision serves as a lighthouse, guiding individuals through the complex and often turbulent waters of financial decision-making. It is the force that propels them forward, providing clarity and direction. With this clear vision in mind, one can set ambitious goals, breaking them down into manageable steps.

Abundance Mentality to embrace the wealth mindset, one must shed the scarcity mentality that fosters fear and competition. Instead, individuals with a wealth mindset believe in the inherent abundance of opportunities and resources in the world. They understand that success is not a zero-sum game and that wealth can be created and shared. This shift in perspective allows for collaboration and a positive outlook, essential for attracting financial opportunities.

Continuous Learning

In a rapidly evolving financial landscape, knowledge is power. The wealth mindset thrives on a commitment to continuous learning. It's about staying curious and open to new ideas and strategies. Whether through books, seminars, or online courses, individuals with this mindset seek to enhance their financial literacy continually.

Risk and Resilience

Financial success often involves taking calculated risks. The wealth mindset acknowledges that setbacks are part of the journey but doesn't falter in the face of adversity. Instead, it thrives on resilience and adaptability. Setbacks become opportunities for growth and learning, not reasons to give up.

Goal Setting and Planning

Turning a vision into reality requires concrete goals and a strategic plan. The wealth mindset is marked by discipline and a commitment to goal-setting. It recognizes that without a roadmap, achieving financial success becomes a mere dream. By setting clear, measurable, and achievable objectives, individuals create a path to follow.

Investment in Self

Perhaps the most valuable asset on the road to financial success is oneself. The wealth mindset emphasizes the importance of investing in personal growth, health, and education. A strong, healthy, and educated individual is better equipped to seize financial opportunities and navigate challenges effectively.

Embrace Delayed Gratification

One of the pillars of the wealth mindset is the ability to delay gratification. Instead of seeking immediate pleasures, individuals make choices that benefit their future selves. This might mean forgoing short-term indulgences in favor of long-term financial security and success.

Positive Affirmations are powerful tools for reprogramming the subconscious mind. The wealth mindset relies on positive self-talk and affirmations to boost self-belief and motivation. Regularly affirming financial goals and capabilities helps maintain focus and determination.

Financial Discipline

A key element of the wealth mindset is financial discipline. This means practicing prudent budgeting, saving, and investing. It involves distinguishing between needs and wants and allocating resources wisely. Financial discipline is the backbone of sustainable wealth creation.

Surrounding Oneself with Success Success breeds success. The wealth mindset encourages individuals to surround themselves with like-minded individuals who inspire and challenge them to reach higher. A supportive network becomes a source of motivation, encouragement, and knowledge-sharing.

Giving Back Surprisingly, one of the secrets to financial success is giving back. The wealth mindset recognizes the importance of contributing to the greater good, whether through charitable acts or mentorship. This not only enhances one's sense of purpose but also fosters goodwill and positive relationships, which can lead to unexpected opportunities.

Wealth mindset is a holistic approach to financial success, encompassing a mindset of abundance, continuous self-improvement, discipline, and resilience. It is a path to not only accumulating wealth but also creating a life rich in purpose and fulfillment. By embracing these principles and incorporating them into daily life, individuals can confidently embark on their journey toward financial success, knowing that their future of prosperity awaits.

OVERCOMING LIMITING BELIEFS

In the quest of mastering the wealth mentality, maybe no challenge is more severe than the limiting ideas that dwell deep inside our brain. These self-imposed constraints may severely hamper our potential to attract prosperity and financial success.

In the pursuit of financial mastery, there exists a profound yet often overlooked obstacle - limiting beliefs. These deeply ingrained thought patterns, often formed in childhood and reinforced over time, can significantly impede one's ability to accumulate wealth and achieve financial success. However, recognizing and conquering these beliefs is a crucial step toward mastering wealth. Let me lead you into exploring the concept of limiting beliefs and offer insights into how they can be overcome on the journey to financial mastery.

The Nature of Limiting Beliefs

Limiting beliefs are self-imposed constraints that shape our thoughts, attitudes, and actions in a way that hinders our progress. These beliefs often manifest in statements such as, "I'm not good with money," "Wealth is only for the lucky few," or "I'll never be rich." They stem from a variety of sources, including upbringing, societal influences, and personal experiences. These beliefs create mental barriers that prevent individuals from realizing their financial potential.

Awareness and Identification

The first step in overcoming limiting beliefs is to recognize and identify them. Often, these beliefs operate subconsciously, driving our decisions without us even realizing it. To become aware of them, one must engage in self-reflection and introspection. Take the time to examine your beliefs about money and wealth. Are they empowering or limiting? Do they support your financial goals, or do they hold you back?

Challenging and Reframing

Once identified, it's essential to challenge and reframe limiting beliefs. This process involves critically examining the validity of these beliefs and replacing them with more empowering alternatives. For example, if you believe, "I'm not good with money," challenge this by seeking financial education and taking practical steps to improve your financial literacy. Reframe it into, "I am continually learning and improving my financial skills."

Cultivating a Growth Mindset

A growth mindset is the belief that abilities and intelligence can be developed through dedication and hard work. Cultivating this mindset is essential in the quest for financial mastery. It encourages the view that skills related to wealth-building can be learned and improved upon over time. By embracing the notion that your financial abilities are not fixed but can grow with effort, you open yourself to endless possibilities.

Positive Visualization and Affirmations

Visualization and positive affirmations can be powerful tools in overcoming limiting beliefs. Visualize your financial goals and imagine yourself achieving them. Affirmations can help rewire your subconscious mind with empowering beliefs. Repeatedly affirm statements like, "I am capable of achieving financial success" or "I attract wealth and abundance."

Seeking Support and Mentorship

Breaking free from limiting beliefs can be a challenging journey, but you don't have to go it alone. Seek support from friends, family, or a therapist. Surround yourself with individuals who inspire and encourage you to challenge your limiting beliefs. Consider finding a mentor who has successfully navigated the path to financial mastery. Their guidance and wisdom can be invaluable.

Taking Action

Ultimately, the most effective way to overcome limiting beliefs is through action. Take tangible steps toward your financial goals, even if they seem small at first. Each small success will chip away at the power of your limiting beliefs and build confidence in your ability to master wealth.

Persistence and Resilience

Overcoming limiting beliefs is not a one-time event; it's an ongoing process. Be prepared for moments of self-doubt and setbacks. Embrace these as opportunities for growth and learning. Maintain your commitment to financial mastery, even in the face of adversity.

By investigating and conquering limiting ideas, you are not only building the road for financial success but also experiencing a fundamental shift in your relationship with money and wealth. This chapter will empower you with the information and skills required to unleash your full financial potential by breaking free from the confines of limiting beliefs.

PART ONE
BUILDING A STRONG FOUNDATION

In the path to financial success, identifying your financial goals and creating specific targets is analogous to drawing a route on a map. Without a target and a well-defined path, reaching financial wealth may be haphazard and unpredictable.

Let me discuss the essential issue of setting your financial goals and developing specific objectives to you:

1. The Blueprint of Financial Success

- Understand why creating financial goals is the cornerstone of a safe financial future.

- Recognize how objectives bring direction, drive, and purpose to your financial pursuits.

2. The Quest for Clarity: Defining Your Financial Goals

- Self-reflection approaches to find your innermost financial ambitions, dreams, and objectives.

- Differentiating between short-term, medium-term, and long-term financial objectives for a comprehensive financial strategy.

3. The Art of Objective Setting: SMART Goals

- Master the SMART criteria: Specific, Measurable, Achievable, Relevant, and Time-bound for developing specific financial targets.

- Crafting your financial objectives should match these requirements, assuring clarity and attainability.

4. Creating a Vision for Financial Success

- Beyond the numbers: the significance of picturing your ideal financial future.

- Harnessing the power of vision to realize your financial ambitions.

5. Sequencing and Prioritizing Your Goals

- Techniques for prioritizing your financial objectives based on significance, urgency, and feasibility.

- Building a step-by-step path to accomplishing your goals.

6. Challenges and Obstacles along the Way

- Strategies for predicting, addressing, and overcoming problems that may emerge throughout your road to financial objectives.

- Maintaining resilience and drive in the face of failures.

7. Tracking Progress and Celebrating Milestones

Implementing a strategy to track your progress toward each financial goal. - The value of recognizing modest triumphs as you move toward greater aspirations.

8. Flexibility and Adaptation

- Recognizing that life circumstances may change, forcing modifications to your financial objectives.

- How to modify and realign your goals while keeping committed to your larger financial strategy.

By mastering the skill of establishing your financial goals and creating specific targets, you obtain the compass and roadmap required to traverse the complicated terrain of financial success. This approach not only delivers clarity and direction but also feeds your enthusiasm to conquer hurdles, eventually helping you transform your financial ambitions into reality.

CHAPTER ONE

DEFINING FINANCIAL GOALS

In the quest of financial success and mastering the wealth mentality, having a clear and motivating vision for your money is key. Your financial vision functions as the guiding light that illuminates the route to your objectives.

TAKE NOTE OF THE FOLLOWING;

1. The Significance of a Wealth Vision

- Understand why a captivating vision is vital for financial success.

- Recognize how a vision offers purpose, drive, and a sense of direction in your financial path.

2. Beyond Dollars and Cents: Defining Your Wealth Vision

- Techniques for introspection to identify your innermost financial objectives and ambitions.

- Exploring the larger elements of wealth, including financial stability, lifestyle, and legacy.

3. Visualizing Your Ideal Financial Future

- The power of imagination in manifesting your financial objectives. - Techniques to vividly create and experience your vision, combining sensory details, emotions, and experiences.

4. Incorporating Values and Principles

- Aligning your financial goal with your own beliefs and ethical ideals.
- Ensuring that your financial ambitions connect with your genuine self.

5. Turning Dreams into Goals

- Translating your wealth vision into precise, practical financial goals. - The importance of goal-setting in bridging the gap between your present financial status and your envisioned future.

6. Making Your Vision Tangible

- Techniques for recording and visualizing your financial vision, such as constructing vision boards or written declarations.

- The advantages of continuously evaluating and improving your vision as you work toward your objectives.

7. Staying Inspired and Motivated

- Strategies for sustaining excitement and concentration on your money goal.

- Utilizing your vision as a source of encouragement through hard times.

8. Building a Legacy

- Considering the long-term influence of your financial goal on future generations.

- Exploring methods to leave a lasting legacy via your financial journey.

By mastering the skill of developing a vision for prosperity, you not only identify your financial goal but also spark the passion and dedication required to accomplish there. Your vision acts as a continual reminder of why you're on this road and helps you handle the problems and opportunities that come along the way, eventually bringing you to a future of financial prosperity and contentment.

CHAPTER TWO

THE GROWTH MINDSET

DEVELOPING A GROWTH MINDSET

While success is essentially defined as the "achievement of intention," a secondary meaning for the phrase is the "attainment of fame, wealth, or power," a pointer to how Americans have predominantly (mis)interpreted the notion. Outer-directed metrics of success have traditionally functioned as the method to assess how successful a person is or isn't, a practice that has worked to the detriment of many of us over the years. Most of us are not famous, rich, or powerful, after all, and even if one does qualify on any of those dimensions, there are always other individuals who possess higher amounts of one or more

Paradigm of success has made a fair percentage of Americans feel less successful than they would otherwise feel if more inner-directed measurements were utilized, I think, and something that has led to much emotional uncertainty and psychological turmoil. We have, for the most part, been utilizing the incorrect type of social currency to quantify or judge achievement, in other words, a contributing cause in our dismal national

Levels of pleasure and well-being. Success in America has mainly been a failure, I maintain a surprising thing considering how much emphasis we devote to the pursuit of it.

There has been a lengthy history of examining the psychology of success in America that supports such a notion. In 1906, Harvard psychologist William James branded Americans' excessive desire as "the exclusive worship of the bitch-goddess success" and "our national disease. "External success is not an infallible indication of internal health," he told a group of medical professionals at the University of Rochester in 1949; his clinical experience revealed that attaining one's professional objectives usually led not to happiness but rather sadness.

Few individuals on the globe understood more about the psychology of success in the early 1960s than David C. McClelland, chairman of Harvard's Department of Social Relations and director of that university's Center for Research in Personality. Making money was part of the incentive to desire to succeed, but there was more to it, he had realized. Americans "enjoyed the sense of challenge and risk and overcoming obstacles and getting somewhere," McClelland noted in 1963, with establishing reasonable objectives as the key to success.

A quarter century later, Steven Berglas had become a major expert on the psychology of success, including its less savory elements. The Harvard Medical School psychologist specialized in what he termed "success-induced disorders" and was the author of The Success Syndrome: Hitting Bottom When You Reach the Top. For Berglas, success might be a "syndrome," a pattern of conduct driven by the typically unrecognized stresses of achievement. There were "victims" of success, he maintained after treating numerous professionals who had crashed and burned after having "made it." Within psychiatric circles, there was now even a term for what Berglas and other psychiatrists were seeing: "self-defeating personality disorder."

After watching more of their workaholic patients beginning to question their aims in life in the 1990s, more psychologists took a closer look at accomplishment and its relationship with mental health. One of them was Stan J. Katz, a Beverly Hills-based clinical and forensic psychologist, who had a great read on the evolving story of success in America. In his private practice, Katz saw more than his fair share of great achievers who seldom had time to appreciate the things for which they worked so hard. "When we were about ending 1990s," he and Aimee E. Liu wrote in Psychology Today in 1992, "we seemed to hit the hollow ground between achieving success and feeling successful," the difference being an essential one.

Psychologist Gilbert Brim argued much the same thing in his 1992 Ambition: How We Manage Success and Failure throughout Our Lives. Success was not an objective metric but a subjective one, the director of the MacArthur Foundation Research Network on Successful Midlife Development stated in the book, and was therefore something that should be reevaluated on a continuous basis. Life changed as one matured, after all, so success at one moment did not ensure it at another. In reality, it was preserving the same measurements of success over time that frequently led to boredom or the sense of failure when one achieved one's maximum potential in a specific profession, he pointed out.

What Abby Ellin named in Psychology Today in 2010 "contender syndrome" was without doubt an unpleasant presence tied to the psychology of success. The notion that one hadn't lived up to one's full potential was a worrisome experience for many, particularly when comparing one's list of accomplishments to those of others. Ellin said that therapists were seeing more individuals suffering from the disease (that referenced to Marlon Brando's character Terry Malloy's classic phrase "I could have been a contender" in the 1954 movie On the Waterfront), a consequence maybe of the comparison nature of social media.

Most lately, the concept that failure is a positive thing has entered the arena of the psychology of success. Some psychologists, career trainers, and consultants have called this notion "failing forward," putting a positive gloss on a personal or professional reversal. One may learn a lot more from failure than success, this idea goes, a reassuring concept to those of us who have not attained the amount of achievement that we had wanted to.

What constitutes actual "success" or "happiness" is a subjective phrase that may vary widely from person to person. What defines success may be depending on one's ideals, desires, and circumstances. The definitions are impacted by different social, personal, and cultural elements. Success in broad terms may be described as the completion of an objective, purpose, or goal. It might be something that you want or manifest for your future.

Success Goals

Achieving achievement involves planning, without which routes cannot be constructed. Human brains need a plan of action to successfully launch and guide meaningful activities towards obtaining the intended objective. Success objectives represent a person's ambitions, which may be aimed towards many parts of life, such work, marriage/ relationships, family, health, personal development, lifestyle, etc. These objectives offer a direction and purpose, which steer people toward the results that they seek. Possessing a SMART goal- Specific, Measurable,

Achievable, Realistic, and Time Bound helps one concentrate on their efforts, and measure their progress as well.

For example, in terms of career, one aims to reach a work position within a given time period, finish a diploma or degree in an area that they wish to succeed in or start a successful enterprise by a certain set date.

In terms of personal growth, one wishes to practice mindfulness and meditation every day to promote emotional well-being and attention.

In terms of finance, one wishes to save a particular amount of money in an emergency fund within a given time period or invest a percentage of income in various investment possibilities to create wealth over time.

Establishing growth Mentality

Psychologist Carol Dweck in her book "Mindset: The New Psychology of Success" developed the notion of growth and fixed mindsets. According to Dweck, tough circumstances may be fatal for individuals with fixed mindsets since they suggest that they don't have the abilities or intellect to finish the work, consequently there are no prospects of any growth. In the contrary, one with a growth mindset thinks that you can develop talents and expertise even if they now don't have them. They feel that talent and intellect may be achieved by one's own work. Learning is a lifetime process, and treating each and every problem as a chance to learn, is the slogan they live by. A person with a development mindset thinks that your past doesn't dictate the route of your progress.

How to Relate to Failure

Dealing with failure is a part of the road towards success. The ability to move through challenging conditions, particularly through setbacks, often known as "resilience" is another major driver of success. The route toward success may resemble a succession of barriers to conquer. When failures come, it may appear that the path to success is fragmenting, yet your existence relies on the capacity to stand up and keep going. The capacity to persist and learn from tough circumstances is a talent needed when coping with failure, and a crucial component of success. Research studies reveal that regular effort, consistency, drive, and discipline are some elements that add up to success in their own possible professional sectors. A good work ethic positions you at a higher likelihood of being promoted, and accomplishing your objectives.

Psychologist Angela Duckworth investigated the idea of "grit" which is a mix of enthusiasm and tenacity in an endeavor to accomplish long-term objectives. The notion of grit argues that without enthusiasm, one who perseveres in anything has higher possibility of coping with burnout. Possessing both passion and persistence offers individuals a mental fortitude that allows them to endure and thrive in the face of adversity. In a TED talk, she emphasized how Grit is like having endurance, staying with your future day in and day out, and living life like it's a marathon rather than a sprint.

Psychological flexibility is another essential towards the route to success. Possessing psychological flexibility involves the capacity to adjust our own behavior to a reality that is continuously changing, as well as the requirements that we find ourselves confronting. Psychologist Crystal Lee in her book "How Rich Asians Think" noted that having this flexibility allows individuals think outside of the box and become innovative when presented with a challenge.

When we investigate the attributes of successful individuals, we discover that they possess A clear vision and are goal-oriented, Are resilient in the face of setbacks, A strong capacity to manage their own urges via self-discipline (and maintain a strong work ethic),

Are devoted to lifelong learning since they have a desire for information, and can adapt to changing conditions and settings.

Risk takers who are prepared to venture out of their own comfort zone and take chances with proper study and preparation

Problem-solving talents where they address difficulties with a rational and innovative perspective.

Leadership abilities where they are able to inspire, encourage and lead others around them, and take a stance before others.

Emotional Intelligence: Successful individuals understand and control their own emotions but also are aware of other's feelings around them, and can sympathize with them. This talent is necessary for efficient communication.

In the midst of hardship, the difference between surviving and succeeding frequently comes down to your perspective. It may have a tremendous influence on how you tackle obstacles and disappointments, your capacity to learn and acquire new skills, personal relationships, and professional success.

The notion of growth and fixed mindsets was conceived by psychologist Carol Dweck, and made famous via her book, "Mindset: The New Psychology of Success". In her studies, Dweck examines the repercussions of assuming that intellect, skill or personality is something that can be learned, rather than being a set quality

Two Mindsets

Fixed mentality

People with a fixed mentality think they were born with a certain degree of intellect, skill, ability - and that's it. It cannot be amended. They desire to seem clever to mask their anxiety of appearing inept to others. They prefer to chronicle their skills, rather than working hard to learn and grow. With this approach, skill leads to achievement, not work and tenacity.

Those with a fixed mentality have a propensity to:

- Avoid challenges

- Give up easy

- See effort as worthless

- Ignore useful negative feedback

- Feel frightened by the success of others

As a consequence, individuals may peak early and accomplish less than their full potential.

Growth mentality

People with a growth mindset think that with enough work and experience, they can become wiser, more competent, and more skilled. Effort has a direct influence on their successes, not skill alone. So they put in the time to study and improve, leading to greater degrees of achievement.

Those with a development mindset are better equipped to:

- Embrace difficulties

- Persist in the face of adversity

- See effort as the route to mastery

- Learn from criticism

- Find lessons and inspiration in the achievement of others

Sake of this, they attain ever-higher degrees of success.

People with a development attitude are not disheartened by failure. In fact, they consider unfavorable events as a chance for self-improvement. Carol Dweck once said: "The passion for stretching yourself and sticking to it, even when it's not going well, is the hallmark of the growth mindset. This is the thinking that permits individuals to survive through some of the most stressful situations of their lives

15 methods to create a development mindset for success

1. Embrace difficulties: View difficulties as opportunities for development and learning rather than barriers.

2. Learn Continuously: Cultivate a passion for learning and attempt to gain new skills and information often.

3. Persist in the Face of Failure: Don't be disheartened by failures; consider them as stepping stones toward development.

4. Effort is Key: Recognize that effort is a route to mastery, and the more you spend in anything, the better you become.

5. Replace "I Can't" with "I Can't Yet": Shift your perspective from fixed to progress by adding "yet" to your restrictions.

6. Seek criticism: Embrace criticism, even if it's critical, since it gives essential insights for growth.

7. Inspire Yourself: Read about the successes of others who have adopted a growth mindset and gain inspiration from their tales.

8. Mind Your Language: Be conscious of the words you use. Avoid negative self-talk and utilize positive affirmations.

9. Set High, Achievable objectives: Challenge yourself with ambitious but achievable objectives that stimulate progress.

10. View Criticism as a Learning chance: Instead of taking criticism personally, consider it as a chance to better your talents.

11. Surround yourself with progress-Minded Individuals: Associate with individuals that encourage your progress and motivate you to be your best.

12. Stay inquisitive: Cultivate an inquisitive mentality by asking questions and striving to understand the "why" and "how" behind things.

13. Adapt to Change: Be adaptable and open to change, as it frequently presents new chances for progress.

14. Visualize Success: Use visualization methods to picture yourself succeeding and attaining your objectives.

15. Appreciate Achievements: Acknowledge and appreciate your victories, no matter how minor, to support your development mentality.

Developing a growth mindset requires time and effort, but it may dramatically boost your chances of success in different facets of life. By implementing these tactics, you may build a mentality that thrives on challenges, learning, and constant progress.

HARNESSING THE LAW OF ATTRACTION
"YOU REAP WHAT YOU SOW AND WHAT YOU THINK IS WHAT YOU GET"

Reaching our objectives demands more than even the greatest genuine resolve. Still, an optimistic outlook counts, and we should take the power of positive thinking seriously.

Your ideas have an influence on your life. Your mentality influences your ideas, behaviors, and actions. Behaviors tend to impact who enters our life and who remains, as a resource or a burden. Your ideas and activities also impact your sentiments about yourself and the world.

Fuelling your thoughts with self-criticism doesn't promote your well-being or create healthy, joyful relationships. And it surely doesn't help you materialize anything better.

On certain days, it's hard to look on the bright side. No one can expect to constantly feel or be optimistic, but a positive mindset helps. So does a growing attitude. Changing how you feel about yourself and the world may influence the way others think about and treat you. That can have concrete effects.

I have personally researched and implemented the LAW OF ATTRACTION in my own life for many years and have boiled it down to the following easy steps:

1) THINK IT

Think fiercely and accurately about what you desire. Be specific. Create a defined picture of that in your mind. Don't worry about how.

2) FEEL IT

Generate the sense of obtaining what you desire with youthful joy. Create the sensation of truly possessing it in your mind and heart. Get emotional! Generate emotions to such a degree that you feel like you truly DO have it.

3) BE GRATEFUL

Be glad for being able to produce precisely what you want, that you have a life that you can fill with beautiful events.

4) DISREGARD NEGATIVE THOUGHTS

Your mind is inclined to focus on the reasons why you won't acquire what you desire. It's OK. It's normal. Simply recognize them and replace them with pleasant ideas. Think on what you want, NOT about what you don't want.

5) TAKE ACTION

Speak about what you desire. Talk to people. Be on the lookout for opportunities. Take activities congruent with truly possessing what you desire.

In the heart of a bustling city, I had always dreamed of mastering the wealth mindset. I was an avid reader and had recently come across a book titled "Mastering the Wealth Mindset," which promised to reveal the secrets of harnessing the law of attraction to create abundance. Intrigued, I decided to embark on a journey of personal transformation that would prove the law of attraction and build my wealth mindset.

I began by setting clear financial goals. I envisioned myself living a life of financial freedom, free from the constraints of debt and financial worries. Every morning, I would spend a few minutes visualizing my goals and feeling the emotions of success, as the book had instructed. I believed that by focusing on these goals with unwavering faith, I could attract the wealth he desired.

One day, as I was walking through the city's crowded streets, I noticed a flyer for a seminar on financial literacy and investment strategies. It was as if the universe had placed this opportunity right in front of me. I eagerly registered for the seminar, convinced that it was a sign that I was on the right path.

The seminar was a revelation. I learned about the power of compounding, the importance of diversified investments, and the value of long-term financial planning. I left the seminar feeling inspired and armed with newfound knowledge. I knew that I needed to take action to align himself with my financial goals.

I began budgeting meticulously and saving a portion of my income every month. I started investing in stocks and bonds, carefully following the principles I had learned at the seminar. I believed that my actions were in harmony with my vision of financial success, and he maintained a positive attitude even in the face of market fluctuations.

As time passed, my wealth began to grow steadily. I received promotions at work, my investments flourished, and unexpected opportunities for additional income came my way. It seemed as though the universe was conspiring to bring me closer to my goals.

One evening, as I reviewed my financial statements and marveled at how far I had come, I realized the profound truth: I had indeed mastered the wealth mindset through the law of attraction. By setting clear intentions, visualizing my goals, and taking deliberate actions, I attracted the abundance I had once only dreamed of.

Here's how I utilized the LOA method to come this far:
1) THINK IT
2) FEEL IT

3) BE GRATEFUL
4) DISREGARD NEGATIVE THOUGHTS
5) TAKE ACTION

At this very minute, your life is being steered and impacted by global forces you may not even be aware of — and the most powerful of them is the Law of Attraction. Just like the rule of gravity, it is constantly in action, touching your life in more ways than you can understand.

The good news is, if you are aware of this universal rule, you can learn how to apply it to alter your life for the better! Because here's the thing: You are in a perpetual state of creation.

Every instant of every day, you are actively shaping your world. With every thought, either consciously or unconsciously, you are constructing your future. And when you know how to harness the power of the Law of Attraction in your life, you can guide your thoughts and actions in a manner that enables you to easily attract what you desire.

Do you doubt the existence of The Law of Attraction?

Many people, when they first hear about this universal rule, reject it as "woo." So if you have concerns about whether it truly works, you're definitely not alone! I regularly receive queries from folks who wonder what the Law of Attraction is and are suspicious about the promises they've heard. And I will let you know what I usually tell them:

Expect wonders.

When you understand how the Law of Attraction works, you can utilize it to transform your life for the better and build a great future.

This book will lead you through the process of employing this powerful universal rule and teach you how to create what you desire in every aspect of your life. I'll educate you about the 7 Laws of Attraction (that's right, there are more than one) and the 3 proven ways to activate it in your life. You'll also learn how to employ it for diverse objectives, like as drawing more prosperity or love into your life.

Buckle up, because it's going to be an awesome journey!

Can you explain the Law of Attraction?

The law of attraction is a universal concept that asserts you will attract into your life whatever you concentrate on. Whatever you devote your focus and attention to is what will come back to you.

When you concentrate on the abundance of good things in your life, you will inevitably attract more positive things into your life. But if you concentrate yourself on negative ideas and solely focus on what you lack in life, then you will eventually draw negativity into your life and what you desire most will continue to evade you.

Do you Know why the Universe uses the Law of Attraction?

Simply explained, it's because like attracts like. If you are feeling eager, energetic, passionate, cheerful, joyous, thankful, or abundant, then you are putting forth good energy to the universe.

In turn, that good energy will attract people, resources, and opportunities that vibrate on the same energetic wavelength. This positivity that is simply introduced into your path of life will assist you to attain your objectives.

On the other side, if you are feeling bored, nervous, stressed out, angry, resentful, or unhappy, you are putting out bad energy. That negative vibe will repel optimism and draw pessimistic individuals and situations into your life.

IDENTIFY THE LAW OF ATTRACTION IN YOUR LIFE

You have undoubtedly seen the law of attraction in your own life. For example, a person who complains all the time generally draws friends or followers who similarly have a negative attitude.

Or joyful and enthusiastic individuals will draw other driven go-getters into their group.

That's the Universal Law of Attraction in action! It's vital to understand that the Universe doesn't care what sort of energy frequency you put out. It doesn't "care" whether you are a good or negative person. It just reacts to what you supply.

By altering your energy frequency, you can change the way the universe reacts to you! You may create certain results in your life simply by generating and leaning into vibrations that coincide with your wishes.

But in order to achieve that, you must become thoroughly and continually aware of your energy, thoughts, and emotions – and the seven various ways in which they influence your world.

THE SEVEN LAWS OF ATTRACTION
1. The Law of Manifestation
In the grand beauty of the universe, there exists a profound principle known as the Law of

Manifestation, a captivating facet of the broader Law of Attraction. It is this very law that can be harnessed as a potent instrument in your journey towards mastering the elusive Wealth Mindset. So, dear reader, allow me to take you on a journey of discovery, as we explore the intricate connection between the Law of Manifestation and your pursuit of financial prosperity.

Imagine, if you will, that the universe is like a magnificent cosmic canvas, responding to the thoughts and desires that emanate from your very being. In this cosmic dance, the Law of Manifestation dictates that your thoughts and intentions hold the power to shape your reality. It is a law that transcends the boundaries of time and space, orchestrating a symphony of events and opportunities to manifest your deepest desires.

At its core, the Law of Manifestation is about aligning your thoughts, beliefs, and emotions with the wealth and abundance you seek. It operates on the principle that like attracts like, echoing the fundamental tenets of the Law of Attraction. By cultivating a Wealth Mindset, you are essentially tuning your consciousness to resonate with the frequency of affluence.

But how, you might wonder, does one practically apply this mystical law in their pursuit of financial mastery? The answer lies in the synergy of several essential elements:

Clarity of Vision: Begin by painting a vivid mental picture of your financial goals. Envision the lifestyle, possessions, and experiences you desire. The Law of Manifestation thrives on clarity; it craves a well-defined target to bring into existence.

Positive Affirmations: Affirmations are your affirming allies in this cosmic journey. Regularly reinforce your belief in your financial potential by repeating positive statements. These affirmations create a harmonious resonance with your wealth aspirations.

Emotional Alignment: Emotions are the fuel that propels your desires into reality. Cultivate feelings of gratitude, abundance, and joy. Feel as if you already possess the wealth you seek, for the universe responds most fervently to the emotions you emit.

Action as Amplification: The Law of Manifestation is not a passive force; it requires you to take inspired action. These actions serve as an amplifier of your intentions, signaling to the universe that you are committed to your wealth goals.

Visualization Rituals: Create a sacred space and time for visualization rituals. In this meditative state, vividly imagine yourself living the life of your dreams, basking in the wealth and abundance you've conjured in your mind's eye.

Detoxify Limiting Beliefs: Identify and release any limiting beliefs or doubts that might act as energetic roadblocks. Consciously replace them with empowering thoughts that reinforce your Wealth Mindset.

As you diligently employ these techniques, you are not merely asking the universe for wealth; you are orchestrating a symphony of intention and action that resonates with the Law of Manifestation. In this beautiful interplay, the universe conspires to bring you opportunities, connections, and resources that align with your financial aspirations.

The Law of Manifestation, in the context of mastering the Wealth Mindset, is a dynamic force that encourages you to become the architect of your financial destiny. It compels you to cultivate a state of mind where wealth is not a distant dream but a tangible reality waiting to manifest.

Let the Law of Manifestation be your guiding star on this transformative journey. Embrace the power within you, align your thoughts and emotions with your financial dreams, and watch in awe as the universe conspires to manifest your wealth in ways that are both magical and grounded in reality. For, in the realm of the Wealth Mindset, the cosmos itself becomes your most faithful co-creator.

2. The Law of Magnetism

The Law of Magnetism, an enchanting concept that complements the Law of Attraction and holds profound relevance in your quest to master the Wealth Mindset. Picture, if you will, the magnetic forces of the universe converging to bring you wealth, success, and prosperity. Let's explore how the Law of Magnetism intertwines with your financial journey, capturing your imagination while remaining firmly grounded in reality.

Imagine the universe as a vast cosmic field of energy, where everything is interconnected through invisible threads of attraction. At the heart of this cosmic web lies the Law of Magnetism, a principle that suggests that like energies attract like energies. It's a magnetic dance where your thoughts, emotions, and actions become magnetic poles, drawing to you the financial abundance and opportunities that resonate with your inner magnetic charge.

Here's how you can harness the captivating Law of Magnetism in your pursuit of mastering the Wealth Mindset:

Polarity of Thought: Your thoughts are the magnetic poles of your financial reality. Focus your mental energy on abundance, prosperity, and financial success. By consistently holding positive thoughts about wealth, you set your magnetic intention into motion.

Emotional Alignment: Emotions are the magnetic currents that amplify your intentions. Cultivate emotions of excitement, gratitude, and confidence in your financial endeavors. These emotions act as a magnetic force field, drawing wealth towards you.

Authentic Alignment: Ensure that your actions and intentions align with your financial goals. When your actions resonate with your true desires, you become a magnetic beacon for opportunities and connections that can propel you towards wealth.

Visualization Rituals: Engage in regular visualization exercises where you vividly picture yourself in a state of financial abundance. This practice strengthens your magnetic attraction to wealth and creates a powerful pull in that direction.

Energy of Giving: The Law of Magnetism operates on the principle of reciprocity. Give generously, whether it's your time, knowledge, or resources. By sending positive energy into the world, you magnetically draw positive energy, including financial abundance, back to you.

Network Synergy: Surround yourself with individuals who share your financial aspirations. Like attracts like, and your network can become a powerful magnet for opportunities, collaborations, and ideas that lead to wealth.

As you diligently apply these principles, you become a magnetic force in the realm of financial abundance. Your thoughts, emotions, and actions align with the magnetic flow of the universe, attracting wealth and prosperity into your life.

The Law of Magnetism, within the context of mastering the Wealth Mindset, is a dynamic and captivating force that beckons you to become a conscious conductor of your financial destiny. It encourages you to align your inner magnetism with your wealth goals, creating a magnetic resonance that draws financial opportunities and success your way.

Dear Reader, let the Law of Magnetism be your guiding compass as you navigate the seas of financial mastery. Embrace the magnetic power within you, align your thoughts and emotions with your wealth aspirations, and watch in awe as the universe orchestrates a magnetic symphony of abundance in your life, enriching both your imagination and your reality. For, in the realm of the Wealth Mindset, you are the master of your magnetic destiny

3. The Law of Unwavering Desire

Do you actually desire the things you feel you want?

The Law of Unwavering Desire is a potent force that goes hand in hand with the pursuit of the Wealth Mindset. Imagine your desire for financial success as a burning flame within your soul, a flame so intense that it cannot be extinguished. It's this unwavering desire that serves as a magnetic force, pulling you closer to your financial goals, even in the face of challenges and adversity. Let's delve into the intricacies of this captivating law, bridging the chasm between imagination and reality.

Envision your unwavering desire as a lighthouse in the darkest of nights, guiding you toward the shores of financial prosperity. It's the tenacity that fuels your ambition and keeps you relentlessly focused on your goals. In the world of wealth mastery, the Law of Unwavering Desire plays a pivotal role, reminding you that your dreams are not mere fantasies but tangible destinations on your life's journey.

Take note of the following points as you embrace the power of unwavering desire:

Crystal-Clear Goals: Begin by setting specific, measurable, and time-bound financial goals. Your unwavering desire thrives on clarity and precision. The more defined your objectives, the stronger your desire becomes.

Burning Passion: Your desire for wealth should be a blazing passion, an unquenchable fire that consumes your thoughts and actions. Cultivate a burning intensity that keeps you focused and resilient in the face of challenges.

Perseverance and Resilience: The path to financial success is rarely a smooth one. In moments of doubt or adversity, your unwavering desire becomes your anchor. It's your commitment to your goals, even when the going gets tough, that sets you apart.

Daily Commitment: Fuel your desire through daily actions and rituals. Each day, take steps – no matter how small – that bring you closer to your financial objectives. Consistency is the key to keeping your desire alive.

Visualize with Conviction: Visualization is a powerful tool. Imagine yourself living your dreams with utmost conviction. Your unwavering desire is strengthened by these vivid mental images, making them more likely to become reality.

Surround Yourself with Inspiration: Seek out sources of inspiration and motivation, whether it's books, mentors, or a supportive community. Let the stories of those who've achieved financial success further fuel your unwavering desire.

In the realm of mastering the Wealth Mindset, the Law of Unwavering Desire is the relentless drumbeat that propels you forward. It reminds you that your desire for wealth is not fleeting but enduring, and that the universe responds to the unwavering intensity of your intent.

As you apply these principles, your unwavering desire acts as a magnet, drawing to you the resources, opportunities, and people who can help you achieve financial success. It's the unwavering commitment to your dreams that sets you on a path to wealth that is not only imagined but ultimately realized.

4. The Law of Delicate Balance

The Law of Delicate Balance is a profound and intricate concept that underlines the pursuit of a Wealth Mindset in a manner that differs from the laws of attraction, magnetism, or unwavering desire. It encourages you to imagine a tightrope walker gracefully navigating their way across the abyss of financial challenges and aspirations. This law emphasizes the importance of equilibrium, precision, and calculated choices as you strive for financial mastery.

Think of the Law of Delicate Balance as the art of walking a fine line, where the financial success you seek is akin to a delicate equilibrium that you must maintain. Here, it's not about the sheer force of attraction but the finesse of harmonizing various elements in your financial journey.

This is what you need to know in applying the law of delicate balance

1. Financial Equilibrium: Recognize that wealth isn't just about accumulating resources; it's about maintaining a balance between income, expenses, and savings. Strive for a balanced financial portfolio that encompasses investments, assets, and liabilities.

2. Risk Management: Financial success often requires taking calculated risks. Balancing your risk tolerance with sound financial decisions is like adjusting the tightrope walker's pole to maintain stability.

3. Adaptability and Flexibility: As the financial landscape changes, so must your strategy. Be agile in adapting to market shifts and changes in your life circumstances. Like a skilled tightrope walker, you adjust your stance as needed to maintain balance.

4. Resilience: Just as a tightrope walker remains poised despite gusts of wind, maintain your financial resilience in the face of setbacks or market fluctuations. Bouncing back from adversity is a key part of the delicate balance.

5. Emotional Balance: Your emotions play a significant role in financial decision-making. Maintain emotional equilibrium, avoiding impulsive decisions driven by fear or greed. A

calm, clear mind is essential for making balanced choices.

6. Long-Term Perspective: Keep your focus on the horizon, much like a tightrope walker who gazes ahead rather than down. Maintain a long-term perspective when setting financial goals and making investments.

The Law of Delicate Balance emphasizes that financial mastery is not about pursuing wealth recklessly but about approaching it with a keen sense of balance. It reminds you that in the pursuit of wealth, every step you take, every choice you make, and every aspect of your financial life should be delicately balanced to maintain stability and progress.

As you incorporate this principle into your financial journey, you'll find that the Law of Delicate Balance guides you to make thoughtful decisions, adapt to changing circumstances, and embrace a holistic approach to wealth mastery. It is the dance of equilibrium that ultimately leads to a life of financial fulfillment, one step at a time.

5. The Law of Harmony

The Law of Harmony, a captivating principle that weaves through your pursuit of the Wealth Mindset, offers a unique perspective on how to achieve financial success. Imagine your financial journey as a beautiful tapestry, where various threads of your life interweave to create a harmonious and prosperous design. The Law of Harmony reminds us that achieving wealth isn't just about accumulating money; it's about creating a symphony of balance and fulfillment.

Consider the concept of a garden, where different plants, each with its unique characteristics, coexist in perfect harmony. In this garden, the Law of Harmony encourages you to nurture the various elements of your financial life to create a flourishing landscape of wealth and prosperity.

Do this to cultivate the Law of Harmony

Align Your Values and Goals: Just as a garden thrives when it's planted in fertile soil, align your financial goals with your core values. This fertile ground serves as the foundation for a harmonious financial journey.

Diversify Your Investments: Like the diverse species of plants in a thriving garden, diversify your investment portfolio. Spread your financial seeds across various assets to minimize risk and maximize growth potential.

Prune Unnecessary Expenses: Much like a gardener prunes dead branches to encourage new growth, trim unnecessary expenses from your budget. This practice allows your financial garden to flourish without unnecessary burdens.

Water the Roots of Debt: When it comes to debt, water the roots wisely. Manage your debt with care, understanding the difference between good debt, which can help your financial garden thrive, and bad debt, which can strangle it.

Balance Work and Life: Just as a garden requires sunlight and shade, balance your career and personal life. Ensure that success in one area doesn't overshadow the other. This equilibrium enhances your overall well-being.

Give Back to Nurture Growth: In your financial garden, giving back is like planting seeds of goodwill. Contribute to charitable causes or support your community, as it not only enriches your garden but also the lives of others.

The Law of Harmony reminds us that achieving a Wealth Mindset is not just about amassing wealth; it's about creating a harmonious financial ecosystem that aligns with our values and principles. By nurturing this harmony, your financial journey becomes a fulfilling and prosperous experience.

6. The Law of Right Action

The Law of Right Action is a profound principle that underscores the idea that our actions play a pivotal role in attracting and manifesting our financial desires. It's a concept that places emphasis on conscious, intentional, and purposeful actions as drivers of financial success. In essence, it suggests that the universe responds not only to our thoughts and emotions but to the choices we make and the steps we take.

Imagine your financial journey as a dynamic process, a continual series of actions that weave together to create the tapestry of your financial life. This law encourages you to be the director of your life's narrative, where each action becomes a pivotal scene in the story of your financial dreams.

The Law of Right Action operates on several key principles:

Alignment with Values and Intentions: Before taking any action, consider whether it aligns with your core values and intentions. Your actions should resonate with your financial goals, ensuring that you are not veering off course but moving steadily towards your desired destination.

Conscious Decision-Making: Financial success is not a random occurrence but a result of conscious and informed decision-making. Evaluate the potential impact of your actions on your wealth-building journey, and make choices that are in line with your goals.

Persistence and Resilience: Just as the most compelling stories feature protagonists who persevere through adversity, your financial journey may encounter challenges. The Law of Right Action urges you to maintain a resilient and persistent mindset, understanding that challenges are part of the narrative that ultimately leads to success.

Learning and Growth: Every action you take, whether it leads to success or presents challenges, is an opportunity for growth and learning. Embrace actions that promote personal and professional development, as they expand your knowledge and skill set, enhancing your ability to attract wealth.

Giving and Receiving: In the grand scheme of financial success, giving and receiving are interconnected. Be open to receiving the abundance that your right actions attract, and reciprocate by giving generously. This harmonious exchange creates a flow of energy that can be incredibly powerful.

Visualizing Success: Visualization is a tool that can complement your actions. Imagine yourself already enjoying the financial abundance you seek. This visualization fuels your actions and serves as a powerful motivator.

The Law of Right Action reminds us that achieving a Wealth Mindset is not just about wishing for wealth but about proactively and purposefully taking steps to make it a reality. Your actions, when fueled by intention, wisdom, and persistence, become the catalyst for attracting the wealth and abundance you desire.

As you continue your journey to master the Wealth Mindset, remember that your actions are not merely day-to-day tasks but the building blocks of your financial destiny. By aligning your actions with your values and goals, taking informed steps, and maintaining resilience in the face of challenges, you set in motion a magnetic force that attracts wealth, opportunities, and prosperity. Your life's story, under the influence of the Law of Right Action, becomes a powerful narrative of financial success and fulfillment.

7. The Law of Universal Influence

The Law of Universal Influence is a compelling concept that plays a significant role in the realm of mastering the Wealth Mindset. It suggests that the universe itself exerts a profound and continuous influence on our lives, affecting our financial circumstances, opportunities, and ultimately, our path to financial prosperity.

Picture the universe as an intricate web, with each strand representing an aspect of our existence. The Law of Universal Influence underscores that every element, from the cosmos to the smallest particle, is interconnected and continuously influencing our reality.

In the context of wealth mastery, this law invites us to recognize that our financial journey is not isolated; it's part of the universal tapestry. As such, it encourages us to harness this universal influence in our favor to achieve financial success.

This is how you can apply the Law of Universal Influence to cultivate the Wealth Mindset:

1. Mindful Awareness: Begin by developing a mindful awareness of the interconnectedness of all things. Understand that every thought, action, and decision you make has a ripple effect in the universal web. By being conscious of this, you can make choices that align with your financial goals.

2. Intention and Energy: The universe responds to your intentions and the energy you emit. Embrace positive intentions and emotions, as they generate a harmonious resonance with your financial desires.

3. Alignment with Natural Laws: Recognize that the universe operates according to various natural laws, such as the law of cause and effect. Align your actions with these laws, and you'll find that they work in your favor, creating a conducive environment for financial success.

4. Giving and Receiving: In the realm of universal influence, giving and receiving are interconnected. Be open to receiving the abundance the universe provides, and reciprocate by giving generously. This balance allows the flow of prosperity to continue.

5. Visualize Success: Visualizations are a powerful tool when harnessed in harmony with the universal influence. Picture yourself already

enjoying the financial abundance you seek, and let these visualizations resonate with the universal web, attracting the opportunities and resources you need.

6. Connect with the Universal Flow: In your pursuit of financial success, align your efforts with the natural flow of the universe. Be patient, and let events unfold in their own time. Trust in the universal influence to guide you towards your goals.

The Law of Universal Influence reminds us that the universe is not a passive backdrop to our lives; it's an active participant. It responds to our thoughts, intentions, and actions. By cultivating an awareness of this interconnectedness and aligning your financial endeavors with the universal influence, you tap into a powerful force that can propel you toward your wealth aspirations.

In your journey toward mastering the Wealth Mindset, remember that the universe itself is a willing collaborator in your quest for financial success. By embracing the principles of the Law of Universal Influence, you can create a harmonious relationship with the cosmos, allowing it to guide you toward the abundance and prosperity you desire.

The Three Hierarchy of Using the Law of Attraction

To activate the power of this global rule, all you have to do is follow a simple three-step process:

*Step 1: **Let the Universe Know What You Want***
Every day, you send out demands to the universe—as well as to your subconscious mind—in the form of ideas. Everything you think about, read about, speak about, and pay

your attention to is telling the universe what you want to attract more of into your life.

That's why it's so vital for you to become more conscious about the ideas you provide to the universe. The clearer and more focused you are on what you actually want, the simpler it will be for you to attract those things into your life.

For example, let's assume you wish to change occupations, relocate to another state, win a big professional award, have your own TV program, or recover from a significant disease.

How would you feel after you've "arrived" at your goal?

What would you be doing during the day?

Who would you be spending time with?

The more you concentrate on what you do want (instead of what you don't want), the quicker you will create your desires and ambitions.

Step 2: **Believe You will receive the things you Want**

It's not enough simply to concentrate on what you want - you have to believe that it's achievable!

If you think about what you want but in your heart you have doubts you will ever get it, you will end up sending confused signals to the universe, which will reply to you with mixed outcomes.

The trouble is, most individuals have limiting ideas that restrict them from inviting plenty and happiness into their life.

If this sounds like you, I advise you to start performing mindset training that will help you release your limiting beliefs and replace them with the idea that you are deserving, valuable, loving, desired, and competent to accomplish any goal you can envision.

Step 3: *Receive What You Want*

Now, to get what you want, you must become a "vibrational match" for what you wish to attract into your life. The best method to achieve it is to develop pleasant sentiments of love, pleasure, admiration, and thankfulness throughout your day.

You might also try feeling the feelings you would be experiencing if you already got what you desired. This will engage your subconscious mind to make those imagined sensations a reality.

Don't forget to take persistent action toward your objectives. Intentions are incredibly strong, but you must take action to receive results!

How to Utilize the Law of Attraction for Targeted Goals

Now let's have a look at some instances of how to apply the law of attraction to materialize certain results in your life.

Attract Money & Financial Success

If you want to build your fortune, spend more time thinking about money!

Read books and watch videos on how to boost your prosperity and generate more money. Envision the precise amount you would desire and by when.

Above all, remember to be grateful for all that you already have and enjoy the richness of everything that's wonderful in your life. This will assist you build a vibrational match for the financial prosperity that you desire in your future.

Love & Relationship Attraction

People who are able to harness the power of the Law of Attraction typically utilize it to attract more love and passion into their life.

Be kind and give with others and yourself. Appreciate the affection you do have in your life and search for methods to exhibit it. The more you produce a vibration of love, the stronger the signal you will send to the Universe and earn greater power to attract love into your life.

Improve Your Well-Being

You may also employ this universal rule to enhance your mental and physical wellness.

Learning how to employ the law of attraction efficiently needs you to become a more positive person who focuses on experiencing soul-enriching feelings such as appreciation, connection, and abundance.

This helps you to create a healthy attitude, which in turn will motivate you to feel more confident and be inspired to take better care of your physical health as well.

Law of Attraction Meditation for Guidance

Meditation is a fantastic type of practice to activate the law of attraction and create a clear, pleasant mind.

Here, try this short meditation exercise to invigorate awareness:

Find a quiet spot, shut your eyes, and concentrate on slowing down your breathing.

Repeat an inspiring word or phrase.

Move into a condition of silence.

If you are new to the practice of meditation, your thoughts may meander and your mind will wander at first. Remember not to be harsh on yourself when this occurs. This is only part of learning how to meditate.

The aim isn't to control your thoughts or attempt to clear your brain of thoughts (both of which are impossible). It's just to become more conscious of your ideas. Once you discover yourself thinking ideas that are unpleasant or don't benefit you, let them go and bring your attention back to the present.

Consistent practice of meditation can help rid your mind of distractions, purify your thoughts, and increase your spiritual connection with the Universe. This will naturally help you be a more optimistic person and attract more good into your life.

Take Action Right Now
Remember these tips:
Your ideas shape your reality: If you want to alter your life, you must start by changing your thinking. When you create an "attitude of gratitude" and teach yourself to concentrate on what's good in life, you will find your life filled with more positive people and events!

Dream big: If you want the Universe to produce large outcomes, you must have big aspirations! Remember, the Universe always reacts to the energy you give forth.

Use positive affirmations: The greatest method to keep your thoughts, actions, and energies focused on your highest objectives is to employ positive affirmations. When you confirm your objectives have already been attained, you stimulate your subconscious mind to make your vision a reality!

Clarify your goals: A clear vision leads to clear outcomes. That's why it's so vital to be straightforward about what you want – and to validate that what you believe you want truly is what you want. Ambiguous wants yield ambiguous consequences.

Use a vision board: Vision boards are a great tool for defining your vision for your life and keeping your objectives front of mind so you can easily attract them into your life.

Part II
BUILDING WEALTH HABITS

While having a high-paying job is a wonderful beginning, many more things are needed if you wish to have a financially secure future. It's crucial to establish wealth building habits to guarantee you're financially secure not only now, but in the years and decades to come.

As Robert Kiyosaki, creator of the Rich Dad Company, argues, "It's not how much money you make, but how much money you keep, how hard it works for you, and how many generations you keep it for."

Pay Yourself First

Paying yourself first doesn't simply apply to those who run companies. It applies to everyone. Frequently, individuals get paid, spend money on bills, and treat themselves to a few nonessentials and then aim to save whatever is left.

Paying yourself first means you automatically channel cash from each paycheck into a savings or investment account.

It's generally feasible to accomplish this via an employment. You may automatically have a part of your income go into an employer-sponsored retirement plan. Sometimes, you may also arrange to have a portion of your salary placed into a conventional savings account.

Without an employer's support, you can opt to simply have automatic contributions from your checking account flow into one or more savings accounts or retirement funds. Treat your savings like loans that you need to pay.

You want to eliminate the temptation to forgo any contributions. Many find it advantageous to have many accounts.

You may automatically have money placed into a retirement account, another amount put into a savings account designated Emergency Fund, and another that is saving for a wedding, home, vacation or any other large purchase.

Develop High Income Skills in a Niche

Your best assets are your knowledge and abilities. The more in-depth your competence is and the more experience you have, the more options are accessible. If you earn more money, you have more to save. Your job is a crucial component in protecting your financial future.

It's crucial to build both in-demand soft talents and hard abilities. Soft skills include interpersonal skills, personality characteristics, attitudes and social and emotional intelligence.

LinkedIn Learning research reveals managers spend 30% more time growing soft skills than ordinary learners.

Hard talents are more teachable and readily assessed abilities. Try upskilling, the process of gaining new skills within your present work role. For example, marketers have to learn how to utilize social media to be relevant in today's digital age.

CHAPTER THREE

Financial Education: The Cornerstone of Wealth Mastery

Understanding Financial Education

Financial education is an indispensable pillar in the realm of personal finance and wealth management. It encompasses a broad spectrum of knowledge and skills that empower individuals to make informed and effective financial decisions. This form of education is essential to achieving financial literacy and a Wealth Mindset, as it equips individuals with the tools needed to navigate the complex world of money and investments.

1. Foundation of Financial Literacy: Financial education provides individuals with the foundation of financial literacy. It imparts fundamental knowledge about concepts like budgeting, saving, investing, and debt management. This foundational knowledge is vital for making sound financial decisions.

2. Risk Management: One of the key aspects of financial education is risk management. It educates individuals about the risks associated with various financial instruments and investments, enabling them to make informed choices based on their risk tolerance and financial goals.

3. Investment Strategies: Financial education delves into various investment strategies and asset classes, from stocks and bonds to real estate and alternative investments. It helps individuals understand the pros and cons of each and how they can align with their wealth-building objectives.

4. Retirement Planning: Understanding financial education is crucial for effective retirement planning. It familiarizes individuals with retirement accounts, such as 401(k)s and IRAs, and teaches them how to save for retirement, manage investments, and create a secure financial future.

5. Debt Management: Many individuals grapple with debt, and financial education provides essential insights into debt management. It covers strategies for reducing and managing debt, including understanding interest rates, credit scores, and consolidation options.

6. Taxation and Legal Considerations: Financial education addresses the impact of taxation and legal regulations on personal finances. It informs individuals about tax-efficient investing, estate planning, and tax implications of different financial decisions.

7. Behavioral Finance: Beyond numbers and equations, financial education explores the psychology of money. It delves into behavioral finance, helping individuals understand their own financial biases and how emotions can influence financial decisions.

8. Economic Awareness: A critical component of financial education is an understanding of economic trends and their impact on personal finances. This knowledge enables individuals to adapt to changing economic conditions and make informed financial choices.

9. Wealth Preservation: Financial education also emphasizes the importance of wealth preservation. It covers strategies for protecting

assets, including insurance, estate planning, and asset allocation to mitigate risks.

10. Continuous Learning: Financial education is an ongoing process. It encourages individuals to engage in continuous learning and stay updated on the latest financial trends and tools. Staying informed is essential for adapting to a dynamic financial landscape.

Financial education is a powerful tool that empowers individuals to take control of their financial futures. It equips them with the knowledge and skills needed to make wise financial decisions, build wealth, and secure their financial well-being. By understanding financial education and actively pursuing it, individuals can embark on a journey towards financial mastery and the realization of their wealth aspirations.

The Importance of Financial Literacy
Financial literacy is like the compass that guides us through the intricate maze of personal

finance, and it holds a paramount significance in our lives. It's not just about managing money; it's the key to unlocking a world of financial opportunities, security, and wealth-building. In this essay, we will explore the multifaceted importance of financial literacy, its profound impact on our lives, and why it is a skill set that everyone should strive to master.

Empowerment and Control

Imagine a life where every financial decision is made with clarity and confidence. Financial literacy grants us this empowerment. It equips us with the knowledge and understanding necessary to take control of our finances. We are no longer passive spectators but active participants in shaping our financial destiny. With this control, we can set and achieve financial goals, build wealth, and secure our financial future.

Informed Decision-Making

The financial world is a complex web of options, from investment choices to insurance policies, credit products, and retirement plans. Without financial literacy, we navigate this labyrinth blindly. However, when we possess financial knowledge, we can make informed decisions. We can evaluate financial products, assess risks, and choose options that align with our personal goals and risk tolerance. Financial literacy is the bridge between confusion and clarity, between uncertainty and informed decision-making.

Budgeting and Saving

Budgeting is often viewed as a tedious task, but it's the backbone of sound financial management. Financial literacy teaches us how to create and manage a budget, enabling us to track our expenses, allocate resources effectively, and save for both short-term and long-term financial goals. It's like having a map that guides us through the financial landscape, helping us make intentional choices.

Debt Management

In a world where borrowing is ubiquitous, financial literacy is crucial for responsible debt management. It educates us about the implications of borrowing, including interest rates, credit scores, and the impact of debt on our financial health. Armed with this knowledge, we can make informed choices about taking on debt, managing existing debts, and ultimately achieving debt freedom.

Investment Knowledge

Investing can be a powerful wealth-building tool, but it comes with its share of complexities and risks. Financial literacy delves into the world of investments, imparting knowledge about various asset classes, investment strategies, and risk management. This knowledge empowers us to make informed investment decisions, diversify our portfolios, and work toward our financial aspirations.

Retirement Planning

Retirement might seem distant, but it's a financial goal that requires careful planning. Financial literacy educates us about retirement accounts, such as 401(k) s and IRAs, and the significance of saving and investing for retirement. It helps us envision a secure financial future and take the steps necessary to achieve it.

Protection and Insurance

Insurance is a critical aspect of financial security, protecting us from unforeseen events. Financial literacy extends to risk management through insurance. It educates us about the types of insurance available, such as health, life, and property insurance, and helps us make informed decisions to safeguard our assets and the well-being of our loved ones.

Tax Efficiency

Understanding the tax implications of financial decisions is crucial for optimizing our financial strategies. Financial literacy teaches us about tax-efficient investing and how to structure our financial affairs to minimize tax burdens, preserving more of our hard-earned money.

Behavioral Finance

Beyond the numbers and equations, financial literacy delves into the fascinating world of behavioral finance. It explores how our emotions and psychological biases can influence financial decisions. This awareness is a key to making rational, well-informed choices and avoiding common behavioral pitfalls.

Economic Awareness

To navigate the shifting sands of personal finance, it's essential to stay informed about economic trends and their potential impact on our financial well-being. Financial literacy keeps us updated on economic conditions and equips us to adapt to changing circumstances.

Life Events Planning

Life is a journey marked by significant milestones—marriage, buying a home, starting a family, and sending children to college. Financial literacy guides us in planning and managing our finances for these various life stages, ensuring we are well-prepared for life's transitions.

Preventing Financial Pitfalls

With financial literacy, we become better equipped to avoid common financial pitfalls. Whether it's overspending, accumulating excessive debt, or making investment mistakes, financial knowledge acts as a protective shield, safeguarding our financial security.

Financial literacy is not just a skill; it's a life-changing tool. It empowers us, guides us, and protects us in the realm of personal finance. It's a skill that opens doors to financial independence, responsible money management, and a secure financial future. In a world where financial decisions have a profound impact on our lives, the importance of financial literacy cannot be overstated. It's a skill set that every individual should strive to master.

Resources for Financial Education

Resources for financial education are invaluable in our quest to become financially literate and master the Wealth Mindset. These resources come in various forms and can be accessed through multiple channels, catering to different learning styles and preferences. In this essay, we'll explore the diverse range of resources available for financial education and how they can contribute to our financial knowledge and well-being.

Books and Publications

One of the oldest and most traditional sources of financial education is books. Countless books on personal finance, investing, budgeting, and wealth-building are available, each offering a unique perspective and insights. From timeless classics like "Rich Dad Poor Dad" by Robert Kiyosaki to contemporary bestsellers, books are treasure troves of financial wisdom.

Financial publications, such as magazines and newspapers like The Wall Street Journal, Forbes, and Money, provide regular updates on financial markets, trends, and insights from experts. These publications offer a wealth of information to stay informed about the ever-changing financial landscape.

Online Courses and Webinars

In the digital age, online courses and webinars have become prominent resources for financial education. Websites like Coursera, Udemy, and edX offer a wide array of courses on topics ranging from personal finance to advanced investment strategies. These courses often feature video lectures, interactive quizzes, and opportunities to connect with instructors and peers.

Webinars hosted by financial experts provide live or recorded sessions that delve into specific financial topics. They offer an interactive platform for learning and the chance to ask questions and receive direct guidance.

Financial Blogs and Websites

Financial blogs and websites are abundant on the internet, offering a continuous stream of financial advice and insights. Bloggers and financial experts share their knowledge on platforms like Investopedia, The Motley Fool, and Nerd Wallet. These resources provide in-depth articles, guides, and tools to help readers understand financial concepts and make informed decisions.

Financial Podcasts
For those who prefer auditory learning, financial podcasts have gained popularity. Podcasts like "The Dave Ramsey Show," "The Clark Howard Podcast," and "Bigger Pockets Money" offer advice, interviews, and real-life stories related to personal finance and wealth-building. These podcasts can be consumed on the go, making them a convenient resource for busy individuals.

Government and Nonprofit Organizations
Government agencies, such as the U.S. Federal Trade Commission (FTC) and the Consumer Financial Protection Bureau (CFPB), provide valuable resources for financial education. These organizations offer guides, toolkits, and information to help individuals understand financial regulations, protect themselves from scams, and make informed financial choices.

Nonprofit organizations, like the National Endowment for Financial Education (NEFE), are dedicated to promoting financial literacy. They develop educational resources and tools for various age groups, including children, teenagers, and adults, to foster financial knowledge and skills.

Financial Advisors and Consultants

For personalized guidance, financial advisors and consultants play a crucial role in financial education. These professionals offer one-on-one consultations, helping individuals create financial plans, manage investments, and make informed decisions tailored to their specific financial goals and situations.

Community Workshops and Seminars

Local community centers and educational institutions often host financial workshops and seminars. These events cover a wide range of topics, from basic budgeting to retirement planning. They offer participants the chance to interact with instructors, ask questions, and learn from experienced professionals.

Financial Apps and Tools

In the era of smartphones, financial apps and tools have gained popularity. Apps like Mint, Personal Capital, and YNAB (You Need a Budget) help individuals track their expenses, create budgets, and manage their financial goals. They provide a practical, hands-on approach to financial education.

CHAPTER FOUR

TAKING CONTROL OF YOUR FINANCES

You just graduated from school and you are indebted to thousands of dollars in student loans, you may be earning 25000 to 30000 every year as a nurse. You might go bankrupt and receive canes of life right?

Not when you have mastered the skills of money management.

Taking control of your financial life is not a one day thing but something to be done daily.

In taking control of your finances, budgeting, debt management, and investments are key areas we need to dive into. Before we take them into details on their own, remember that;

Financial control is not just about managing your money; it's about managing your life. It's the key to unlocking a future of security, freedom, and the ability to pursue your dreams. Let's explore the steps to taking control of your finances and how it can empower you to live life on your terms.

Set Clear Financial Goals

The journey to financial control begins with setting clear, achievable goals. Ask yourself, what do you want to achieve financially? Whether it's buying a home, saving for retirement, paying off debt, or starting a business, having specific goals provides direction and motivation.

Create a Budget

A budget is your financial roadmap. It's the tool that ensures you're in control of your spending and saving. List your income and expenses, allocate funds to various categories, and stick to your budget. It helps you live within your means and avoid unnecessary debt.

Build an Emergency Fund

Life is unpredictable, and financial emergencies can strike at any time. Having an emergency fund, typically three to six months' worth of living expenses, provides a financial safety net. It prevents you from going into debt when unexpected expenses arise.

Manage and Reduce Debt

Debt can be a heavy burden. To take control of your finances, focus on managing and reducing your debt. Start with high-interest debts, such as credit card balances, and work your way down. Pay more than the minimum, and consider consolidation or refinancing to lower interest rates.

Save and Invest

Saving is the foundation of financial stability, while investing is the path to wealth-building. Automate your savings by setting up regular transfers to a savings or investment account. Make informed investment choices based on your risk tolerance and financial goals.

Live Below Your Means

To take control of your finances, it's essential to live below your means. This means spending less than you earn. It not only helps you build savings but also provides financial security. Avoid lifestyle inflation and focus on building wealth.

Stay Informed

The world of personal finance is ever-evolving. Stay informed about financial trends, new investment opportunities, and changes in tax laws. Knowledge is your greatest asset in making informed financial decisions.

Protect Your Assets

Insurance is your shield against unforeseen events. Make sure you have adequate insurance coverage for health, life, home, and vehicles. This protection ensures that an unexpected incident doesn't derail your financial progress.

Plan for Retirement

Financial control extends to your retirement planning. Contribute to retirement accounts, such as 401(k)s and IRAs, and make sure your investments align with your retirement goals. A well-planned retirement secures your financial future.

Seek Professional Guidance

Financial advisors can provide valuable guidance in your journey to financial control. They can help you create a comprehensive financial plan, manage your investments, and make informed decisions.

Avoid Impulse Purchases
Impulse purchases can derail your budget and financial control. Be someone who is mindful of what you buy. Consider if the purchase aligns with your financial goals and if it's a need or a want.

Track Your Progress
Consistently track your progress and check your goals. Celebrate your achievements. This ongoing assessment keeps you on the path to financial control.

Teach Financial Literacy
Share your knowledge of financial control and literacy with your family. Educate your children

about money, budgeting, and wise financial decisions. Passing on this knowledge ensures a legacy of financial responsibility.

Taking control of your finances is a journey that leads to financial freedom and the ability to shape your life as you desire. By setting clear goals, managing your budget, saving, and investing wisely, you can achieve financial control and build a secure future. It's not just about money; it's about the power to live life on your own terms.

CHAPTER FIVE

INVESTING FOR WEALTH

Investing can be called Wealth Multiplication in one way or the other. Investing allows your money to grow over time through the magic of compounding. Imagine you invest $10,000 in stocks that generate an average annual return of 7%. In the first year, you'd earn $700. But in the second year, you don't just earn $700 on your initial $10,000; you earn $700 on the $10,700 you had after the first year. Over time, this compounding effect significantly multiplies your initial investment.

After 20 years at a 7% return, your initial $10,000 would grow to nearly $39,000. This growth is the result of your money working for you and generating returns on the returns it previously earned.

Beat Inflation: Inflation is the silent wealth eroder. Let's say you have $100,000 today, but the inflation rate is 3%. In a year, your $100,000 will only have the purchasing power of $97,000. However, investments can potentially outpace this rate.
If your investments return 5% annually, your $100,000 would grow to $105,000 in a year, outpacing inflation and preserving or increasing your wealth's real value.

Diversification: Diversifying your investments is like planting a variety of crops in your financial garden. If one crop doesn't perform well, others can compensate. For example, stocks, bonds, real estate, and commodities may perform differently in different market conditions. By spreading your investments across these asset classes, you reduce the risk of significant losses.

During a recession, stocks may decline, but bonds may provide stability or even appreciate in value, balancing your portfolio's performance.

Financial Freedom: Successful investments can create passive income streams. For instance, if you own rental properties, you receive rental income regularly without active effort. This passive income can cover your expenses, giving you the freedom to pursue your passions or other investments.

Rental income from real estate investments can provide ongoing financial security and enable you to focus on other pursuits or retirement without worrying about active employment.

Long-Term Growth: Investing encourages a long-term perspective. Market fluctuations occur, but over time, markets tend to appreciate. This long-term view helps you ride out short-term volatility and benefit from the overall growth of your investments.

Example: Consider the historical performance of the stock market; despite occasional downturns, it has shown steady growth over decades, creating wealth for long-term investors.

Retirement Planning: Investing is a fundamental aspect of building a comfortable retirement fund. By consistently investing a portion of your income, you ensure you have the financial means to maintain your desired lifestyle in retirement.
Regular contributions to retirement accounts like a 401(k) or IRA can accumulate over your working years, providing a nest egg for retirement.

Entrepreneurial Ventures: Investing can fund entrepreneurial endeavors. If you have a business idea or want to expand an existing one, investments can provide the necessary capital for growth and wealth creation.

A tech startup may seek investment from venture capitalists to fund product development and marketing, potentially leading to significant financial returns.

Legacy Building: By accumulating wealth through investments, you can create a financial legacy for future generations. For example, you can set up trusts, endowments, or foundations that benefit your family or charitable causes.

For instance the Rockefeller family's wealth was built through investments and, in part, used to establish the Rockefeller Foundation, which has made a profound impact on global health and education.

Investing is the process of nurturing your financial resources over time, protecting them from the erosive effects of inflation, and nurturing their growth potential. Through diversification, passive income, and a long-term perspective, it can pave the way to financial security, independence, and a lasting legacy.

Types of Investments:

1. Stocks: When you invest in stocks, you're essentially buying a share of ownership in a company. Stocks offer the potential for significant returns but also come with higher risk due to market volatility.

Factors to Consider:

Company fundamentals: Assess the financial health, growth prospects, and industry of the company.

Risk tolerance: Understand your willingness to bear market fluctuations.

Investment horizon: Consider how long you plan to hold the stocks.

2. Bonds: Bonds represent debt securities issued by governments or corporations. When you invest in bonds, you're essentially lending money in exchange for periodic interest payments and the return of the principal.

Factors to Consider:

Credit quality: Evaluate the issuer's creditworthiness.

Yield and maturity: Determine the interest rate and the bond's term.

Market conditions: Monitor interest rate trends that affect bond prices.

3. Real Estate: Real estate investments involve buying physical properties or real estate investment trusts (REITs). Real estate can generate rental income and potential appreciation.

Factors to Consider:

Location and property type: Choose properties in desirable areas.

Market conditions: Assess the real estate market's health and trends.

Maintenance and management: Consider costs and time involved.

4. Mutual Funds: Mutual funds pool money from various investors to invest in a diversified portfolio of stocks, bonds, or other assets. They offer diversification and professional management.

Factors to Consider:

Investment objective: Select funds aligned with your goals.

Expense ratio: Evaluate the fees associated with the fund.

Past performance: Consider historical returns but not as the sole indicator.

5. Exchange-Traded Funds (ETFs): ETFs are similar to mutual funds but trade like stocks on an exchange. They provide diversification and liquidity.

Factors to Consider:

Tracking index: Understand the benchmark the ETF follows.

Liquidity: Assess the ETF's trading volume.

Expenses: Compare ETF fees to ensure cost-effectiveness.

6. Commodities: Commodities include physical assets like gold, oil, or agricultural products. They can serve as hedges against inflation and diversify a portfolio.

Factors to Consider:

Supply and demand: Analyze factors affecting commodity prices.

Storage and costs: Consider storage and transaction costs.

Economic conditions: Evaluate how economic conditions impact specific commodities.

7. Savings Accounts and CDs: These are low-risk, low-return options offered by banks. Savings accounts provide easy access to funds, while certificates of deposit (CDs) offer higher interest rates with a fixed term.

Factors to Consider:

Interest rates: Compare rates offered by different banks.

Liquidity needs: Determine how easily you need access to your money.

FDIC insurance: Ensure deposits are insured for safety.

Factors to Consider Before Choosing an Investment:

1. Risk Tolerance: Assess how comfortable you are with potential losses. Riskier investments often offer higher returns but come with greater volatility.

2. Investment Goals: Define your financial objectives, whether it's short-term gains, long-term growth, income, or a combination.

3. Time Horizon: Consider how long you intend to invest. Longer time horizons can accommodate riskier investments.

4. Diversification: Spread your investments across different asset classes to reduce risk.

5. Market Research: Understand the current economic and market conditions, and stay informed about the investments you're considering.

6. Fees and Costs: Be aware of management fees, transaction costs, and how they affect your returns.

7. Tax Implications: Assess how taxes will impact your investment returns.

8. Liquidity Needs: Determine how easily you need to access your invested funds.

9. Financial Knowledge: Ensure you understand the investment type and its associated risks.

10. Professional Advice: Consider consulting a financial advisor for personalized guidance.

Your choice of investment should align with your financial situation, goals, and risk tolerance. It's crucial to conduct thorough research and make informed decisions to build a diversified and balanced investment portfolio.

INVESTMENT RISK MANAGEMENT

Risk is an inherent aspect of life, and when it comes to investments, it's a fundamental consideration. To manage risk effectively, let's explore this concept through the lens of a renowned individual's life experience: Warren

Buffett, one of the world's most successful investors. By delving into his story, we can glean valuable insights into how he has managed risk throughout his investment journey.

Warren Buffett's life and investment approach are emblematic of a man who, despite his enormous wealth, has always emphasized the importance of risk management. His story offers us a valuable lesson on the essence of prudently dealing with risk.

Warren Buffett's investment philosophy is often distilled into a single word: value. He has built his fortune by investing in companies with strong fundamentals, substantial cash flows, and long-term potential. This approach inherently addresses the risk factor. By focusing on businesses with a competitive advantage and trustworthy management, Buffett has consistently reduced the risk of significant financial losses.

Buffett's emphasis on the "margin of safety" further illustrates his approach to risk management. He advises investors to buy stocks when their market price is significantly lower than their intrinsic value. This discount acts as a cushion against potential market downturns. By not overpaying for stocks, he shields his investments from excessive risk.

Aside that, Warren Buffett's aversion to unnecessary complexity is a testament to his risk-averse nature. He famously states, "Never invest in a business you cannot understand." This advice is invaluable for the average investor. It underscores the importance of investing in assets you can thoroughly comprehend. Avoiding overly complex financial instruments reduces the risk of making ill-informed decisions.

Buffett's life story serves as a prime example of the significance of a long-term perspective in risk management. He has consistently advised investors to focus on the enduring value of their investments rather than reacting to short-term market fluctuations. By resisting impulsive decisions and holding onto solid assets, he mitigates the risk of making hasty, emotionally driven choices.

Warren Buffett's diversification strategy, though often attributed to him, might be somewhat surprising. He advocates for a more concentrated portfolio, arguing that diversifying too widely can dilute the potential for substantial returns. However, his emphasis on this approach stems from his profound understanding of the businesses he invests in. While he maintains a concentrated portfolio, he knows these companies inside and out, thus reducing the risk associated with broad diversification.

What I am trying to say is, Warren Buffett's life and investment journey offer a compelling case study in risk management. His emphasis on fundamental value, a margin of safety, simplicity, a long-term perspective, and concentrated investments illuminates the path to success while mitigating the hazards inherent in the investment world.

So, in the context of investing for wealth, it's imperative to draw inspiration from Buffett's wisdom. Understand the assets you invest in, seek a margin of safety by not overpaying, embrace a long-term perspective, and balance diversification with in-depth knowledge. By incorporating these principles into your investment strategy, you can effectively manage risk and steer your financial journey towards prosperity, just as Warren Buffett has done over his remarkable lifetime.

Investment strategies are the approaches and methods you use to manage your investments effectively. Let's look at some investment strategies

1. Buy and Hold: This strategy involves purchasing investments and holding onto them

for an extended period, often years or even decades. The goal is to benefit from the long-term growth potential of the assets.

Key Point: It's a patient strategy that relies on the natural appreciation of investments over time, such as stocks or real estate.

2. Dollar-Cost Averaging: With this strategy, you invest a fixed amount of money at regular intervals, regardless of market conditions. This approach can help smooth out the impact of market volatility.

Key Point: It reduces the risk of making large, poorly timed investments and is a disciplined way to accumulate assets.

3. Value Investing: Value investors look for undervalued , such as stocks or real estate, based on fundamental analysis. They seek to buy assets for less than they believe they're worth.

Key Point: The goal is to capitalize on the assets' potential to appreciate when the market realizes their true value.

4. Income Investing: Income investors prioritize assets that generate regular income, like dividend-paying stocks, bonds, or rental properties.

Key Point: This strategy aims to provide a consistent cash flow, often suitable for retirees or those seeking passive income.

5. Growth Investing: Growth investors focus on assets with the potential for significant capital appreciation, even if they don't provide immediate income.

Key Point: The goal is to benefit from the asset's value increasing over time.

6. Market Timing: Market timing involves trying to predict market movements and making investment decisions based on those predictions.

Key Point: It can be risky and challenging, as it relies on forecasting market trends accurately.

7. Diversification: Diversification is about spreading your investments across different asset classes to reduce risk. This can include a mix of stocks, bonds, real estate, and other investments.

Key Point: It's a risk management strategy to avoid having all your eggs in one basket.

8. Index Investing: Investors following this strategy aim to match the performance of a market index, such as the S&P 500. They invest in index funds or exchange-traded funds (ETFs) that replicate the index.

Key Point: It's a low-cost, passive strategy that provides broad market exposure.

9. Retirement Planning: This strategy involves saving and investing for retirement. It often includes employer-sponsored retirement

accounts like 401(k)s and individual retirement accounts (IRAs).

Key Point: It's about accumulating enough funds to maintain your desired lifestyle in retirement.

10. Active vs. Passive Investing: Active investors try to outperform the market by making frequent buying and selling decisions. Passive investors aim to match market returns with minimal trading.

Key Point: Actively managed strategies involve more hands-on management and often higher fees.

11. Risk Management: This strategy focuses on assessing your risk tolerance and adjusting your investments accordingly. Conservative investors may choose safer assets, while aggressive investors may opt for higher-risk opportunities.

Key Point: It's essential to align your investments with your comfort level regarding potential losses.

12. Tax-Efficient Investing: Tax-efficient investors aim to minimize their tax liabilities by utilizing tax-advantaged accounts and strategies.

Key Point: Reducing taxes can significantly impact your after-tax returns and overall wealth.

Remember that the right investment strategy for you depends on your individual financial goals, risk tolerance, and time horizon. A well-thought-out strategy should align with your objectives and be flexible enough to adapt to changing circumstances. It's often advisable to seek guidance from financial professionals to develop and implement the right strategy for your specific situation.

Financial planning is like setting a roadmap for your money. It's about making sure you have enough funds for today and tomorrow. Investing is a key part of that plan.

Think of it this way: you have short-term needs like bills and groceries, but you also have long-term goals, like retirement or buying a home. Investing helps you grow your money for those long-term goals.

For example, if you put some money into a retirement account every month, that's investing. Over time, it grows, and when you're ready to retire, you'll have a nice nest egg.

So, financial planning is about balancing your short-term and long-term needs, and investing is the tool that helps you achieve your long-term financial dreams. It's like planting seeds today to enjoy a bountiful harvest in the future.

PART THREE
Overcoming Obstacles for Success

Success is seldom a smooth, obstacle-free route. Instead, it typically means experiencing many hurdles and disappointments along the route. How you address these hurdles may dramatically affect your eventual achievement. This is what you need to know in your journey to overcoming difficulties for success:

1. Understanding the Nature of Obstacles
Recognize that hurdles are a natural component of every meaningful endeavor. – Understand that challenges may come in numerous forms, including external and internal impediments.

2. Resilience and Perseverance
Develop resilience, which is the capacity to bounce back from hardship.
Cultivate an attitude of persistence, where you stay motivated and devoted even while encountering setbacks.

3. Problem-Solving Skills
Hone your problem-solving ability to approach challenges systematically.
 Break down big issues into smaller, doable tasks.

4. Acknowledging Failure as an Opportunity to gain experience

See failure not as a dead-end but as a wonderful source of learning and progress.

Analyze failures to uncover lessons and insights that may lead to future success.

5. Seeking Support and Guidance

Don't hesitate to seek guidance and help from mentors, coaches, or peers.

Collaborative problem-solving may frequently lead to new solutions.

6. Adaptability and Flexibility

Be open to change and adaptive in the face of unanticipated obstacles.

Adjust your methods and plans as required to overcome problems.

7. Maintaining Focus on Goals

Keep your long-term objectives in mind to remain motivated through hard times.

Use your ambitions as a source of motivation to push through challenges.

8. Emotional Resilience

Develop emotional intelligence to handle tension, worry, and other emotions that may develop while coping with problems.

Practice self-care and stress reduction practices.

9. Positive Mindset

Maintain a cheerful and hopeful mindset, especially while confronting hardship.

Cultivate a conviction in your abilities to overcome obstacles.

10. Learning from Others

Study the experiences of successful persons who have confronted and overcame problems.

Draw inspiration from their experiences and methods

Overcoming barriers is not only a vital component of the route to success but also a critical feature of personal growth and development. By acquiring the skills and mentality to manage problems successfully, you may convert hurdles into stepping stones toward attaining your objectives and fulfilling your vision of success.

CHAPTER SIX

OVERCOMING FEAR AND FAILURE

MANAGING THE FEAR OF FAILURE

The fear of failure may be a huge obstacle to achievement, sometimes holding people back from following their goals and desires. Learning to control and conquer this anxiety is vital for personal and professional progress.

Reframe Your Perspective on Failure
Understand that failure is not the end but a part of the route to success.

View failure as a wonderful learning experience that may lead to development and progress.

Failure is actually an opportunity to learn. The more you fail, understand that the more you stand the chances of winning.

Set Realistic Expectations
Avoid establishing excessively high demands for yourself. You have to understand that nothing good comes on a silver platter and you cannot use a day to build a magnificent temple. Do not built castles in the air and be realistic. Have expectations that suits your environment.

Recognize that failures and errors are common and not indicative of your value.

Embrace a Growth Mindset
Cultivate a mentality that embraces difficulties and views effort as a road to mastery.
Believe in your capacity to learn, adapt, and grow over time.

Identify and Challenge Negative Beliefs
Explore and face any limiting ideas or self-doubt that contribute to your fear of failing.
Replace negative ideas with positive affirmations and motivating beliefs.

Break Down Goals into Smaller Steps
Divide your ambitions into simple, doable activities.
Smaller milestones are less scary and create a feeling of success.

Focus on the Process, Not Just the Outcome
Shift your emphasis from the final product to the time and devotion you put into the process.
Concentrate on what you can control, such as your actions and tactics.

Develop Resilience
Strengthen your capacity to bounce back from failures and hardship.
Embrace adversities as chances to improve resilience.

Seek Support and Encouragement
Share your aims and anxieties with trustworthy friends, family, or mentors.
Their support and encouragement may give a crucial boost in confidence.

Celebrate Small Wins
Acknowledge and appreciate your victories, no matter how minor.

Recognizing your progress promotes self-esteem and decreases the fear of failure.

Practice Self-Compassion

Treat yourself with the same love and empathy you would give a friend.

Avoid severe self-criticism and self-judgment.

Take Action despite Fear

Recognize that fear is a normal feeling, but it shouldn't immobilize you.

Take action even when you feel terrified, since bravery is not the absence of fear but the determination to act in spite of it.

Managing the fear of failure is a continuous process that requires self-awareness, self-compassion, and a commitment to personal improvement. By applying these tactics, you may progressively minimize the influence of anxiety on your quest of success and unleash your full potential. Remember that failure is not a destination but a stepping stone on the route to accomplishment.

CALCULATED RISK-TAKING

In both personal and professional undertakings, taking risks is frequently an essential step toward reaching meaningful objectives and experiencing success.

Understand the Nature of Risk

Recognize that risk is an integral component of life and achievement. Avoiding any risk might restrict your possibilities for development and accomplishment.

Weigh the Pros and Cons

Evaluate the possible rewards and downsides of the risk you're contemplating.
Consider the short-term and long-term repercussions.

Define Your Risk Tolerance

Assess your comfort level with risk and assess how much uncertainty you can handle. Your risk tolerance might vary depending on the individual event and your unique circumstances.

Gather Information

Research and acquire as much information as possible on the danger you're contemplating. – Knowledge may help you make educated judgments and eliminate ambiguity.

Set Clear Objectives

Establish clear and explicit objectives relating to the risk you're taking.

Having a stated purpose may guide your activities and help you gauge success.

Develop a Contingency Plan

Anticipate alternative outcomes and build a contingency plan for each situation.

Be prepared to adapt and react to unanticipated difficulties.

Start Small

If you're new to risk-taking, try beginning with smaller, controllable risks.

Gradually improve your confidence and experience.

Seek Advice

Consult with mentors, advisers, or specialists who have expertise in the area of risk you're studying.

Gain insights from their experiences and viewpoints.

Trust Your Intuition

Listen to your gut thoughts and intuition while making decisions. – Sometimes, your intuition may give helpful counsel.

Diversify Your Risks

Avoid throwing all your energy or efforts towards a single risk. – Diversifying your risks may help spread possible losses and boost your chances of success.

Monitor and Adjust

Continuously analyze the development and outcomes of your risk-taking activities.

Be open to alter your plan depending on comments and results.

Embrace Failure as a Learning Opportunity

Understand that not all risks will lead to success, and failure is a possibility.

 Treat failure as a positive learning experience and a chance for progress.

Celebrate Your Successes

Acknowledge and appreciate your triumphs and successful risk-taking activities.

Recognizing your successes may increase confidence and drive.

Calculated risk-taking is about making educated choices that balance the potential for benefit with the likelihood of loss. It entails rigorous preparation, a willingness to learn from both success and failure, and a dedication to pursue meaningful objectives despite uncertainty. By mastering the skill of judicious risk-taking, you may open doors to new possibilities and achieve greater success in numerous facets of your life.

CHAPTER SEVEN

DEALING WITH SETBACKS

As one of the creators of Clasp, I've witnessed and talked to hundreds of enthusiastic, well-intentioned individuals who are thrilled to alter their financial life. But what happens when life goes off track?

We're all wrestling with that topic today more than ever before as the whirlwind that is 2020 draws to a conclusion. This year marks the second global economic catastrophe that we've been dealing with in only a decade. And for millennials in particular, suffering two such disastrous disasters during key financial years is proving to be catastrophic to asset accumulation. The cold hard reality is that it is difficult to forecast unexpected occurrences, else they would be expected, right? But as the phrase goes, while establishing any plan expect for the best but prepare for the worse.

Sometimes however, the unexpected might be so terrible that it entirely derails and debilitates you. In these instances, when it all appears so daunting and how can we overcome inertia and go forward?

The key to coping with financial failures is retaining perspective and healing the harm to our attitude. No one appreciates bad setbacks – in fact when we do confront them, we frequently feel absolutely helpless and it may seriously hurt our whole vision of the world.

But the trick here is to cure our thinking, and here's how: Create space around your situation Oftentimes we acquire these established mental models of how we feel the world should function. And when unfavorable scenarios develop that vary from what we feel should happen, it might damage our mental health.

Acknowledge that many things are actually beyond your control. Allowing for distance between your circumstances and your identity is crucial. Don't bind yourself to your financial conditions. You are more than your financial balance. Repeat after me: "My self-worth is not my net worth.

Give yourself a rest

Let's face it. Our financial condition is as much impacted by our own personal decisions as it is by bigger systemic forces. Acknowledging and accepting this fact may relieve us of the guilt frequently connected with financial disappointments and eventually help us to get off the success treadmill.

It's normal to revise your objectives to reflect reality and there should be no guilt in doing so. For example, if you're anxious about not achieving a savings target, decrease the goal in half. Or give yourself permission to put the aim on wait. . Create a supportive atmosphere

Perspective is how you interpret the world around you. Building a supportive atmosphere keeps you grounded at times when you feel overwhelmed and helps you to create relationships to people. Try cleaning up your digital surroundings by following outstanding financially-focused influencers that you can connect to. Or join an online group that supports open conversation, where you may learn from others as well as offer your own experience.

But remember, it's crucial to spend the time in choosing the proper people to surround yourself with, whether it's who you follow on social media or who you phone late at night when you're up fretting about your money troubles. Your mentors should represent your ideals and who they are as a person.

When everything is said and done, the key to financial health is mental health. Start by being patient with yourself and set the scene to better keep perspective in order to overcome setbacks. And above all, realizing that a financial setback is just as devastating to your mental health as it is to your net worth is an essential step in getting back on track.

Nurturing the Skills That Unleash Financial Abundance

Manifesting money is more than simply a desire; it's a comprehensive technique that requires matching your ideas, actions, and goals to attract prosperity into your life.

1. Visualization and Manifestation Techniques: Visualize your financial objectives as already attained. Manifestation methods, like vision boards, meditation, and scripting, may help you concentrate your energy and intention on attracting money.

2. Mindfulness and Positive Affirmations: Practice mindfulness to remain present and cheerful. Incorporate affirmations that strengthen your belief in prosperity and riches. Replace self-limiting beliefs with powerful words.

3. Law of Attraction Mastery: Understand and implement the concepts of the Law of Attraction. This universal rule implies that like attracts like. Align your ideas,

emotions, and actions with the energy of riches and plenty.

4. Instincts and Gut Feelings: Trust your instincts while making financial choices. Gut sensations can give information that intellectual reasoning may overlook. Cultivate self-awareness to tap into your intuition more effectively.

5. Gratitude Journaling: Regularly write down things you're thankful for. Gratitude turns your emphasis from lack to abundance, allowing more wonderful events into your life.

6. Visualization of Abundant Lifestyle: Imagine yourself enjoying the life you choose, with all the financial freedom you wish. Feel the feelings connected with that lifestyle, since this emotional alignment may hasten manifestation.

7. Detachment and Letting Go: Strive for a balance between intention and detachment. Set your goal to materialize money, but avoid getting obsessive or

desperate. Trust the universe's timing and let go of the result.

8. Energy Management: Your energy determines what you attract. Practice things that improve your vibrational frequency, such as exercising, spending time in nature, and indulging in hobbies you enjoy.

9. Consistent Grind and Action: While energy and mentality are necessary, taking consistent action is as critical. Put effort into money-making efforts, matching your actions with your aspirations.

Visualization of Giving Back: Envision how you'll contribute constructively to the world when you enjoy financial wealth. Visualizing how you'll benefit others will boost your manifestation efforts.

CHAPTER EIGHT

THE WEALTH OF RELATIONSHIPS

Success typically depends on the relationships you establish, and having a supporting network may greatly assist to attaining your objectives.

Identify Your Goals and Needs

Determine your precise objectives and areas where you want help or expertise.

Understanding your requirements will help you in developing a personalized network.

Cultivate Strong connections

Prioritize quality over quantity when developing connections.

Invest time and effort in cultivating friendships that are authentic and meaningful.

Seek Mentors and Role Models

Look for those who have attained the achievement you desire to.

Mentors and role models may give direction, counsel, and inspiration.

Be a Giver, Not Just a Taker

Actively contribute to your network by giving aid, support, and knowledge.
Building reciprocal ties promotes trust and grows your network.

Attend Networking Events

 Participate in industry-specific events, conferences, and seminars. - These meetings are fantastic chances to meet like-minded folks.

Join Professional Organizations

Become a member of organizations related to your profession or interests. - These clubs generally offer networking opportunities and information.

Utilize Social Media

Leverage social media networks like LinkedIn to engage with experts in your sector.

Share your expertise and participate in discussions to build your online network.

Build a Diverse Network
Seek contacts from varied backgrounds, sectors, and opinions.
Diversity in your network may give new perspectives and possibilities.

Attend Workshops and Mastermind Groups
Participate in workshops or mastermind groups that foster cooperation and brainstorming. - These surroundings stimulate creativity and problem-solving.

Maintain and Nurture Relationships
Regularly remain in contact with your network members. Show thanks for their support and efforts.

Be Open to Learning
Approach your network with an attitude of constant learning.

Be attentive to fresh ideas and comments from your contacts.

Be Clear About Your Expectations

Communicate your aims and what you intend to accomplish via your network.

Clarity helps people understand how they may aid you.

Support Others' Success

Celebrate the successes of your network members.

Offer aid when they need it, building a mutually supportive atmosphere.

Engage in provide-and-Take Relationships

Be open to both provide and accept help.

A network grows when members give and receive in return. Be Patient and Persistent Building a strong network requires time and effort.

Be patient and diligent in building and keeping your relationships.

A helpful network may give direction, chances, and a feeling of belonging on your route to success. By actively creating and maintaining your network, you may tap into a vital resource that can drive you toward your objectives and help you overcome hurdles along the way.

Leveraging Connections for Success

Building a network of meaningful contacts is a critical step, and understanding how to leverage these relationships successfully to accomplish your objectives is also vital.

Clearly Define Your Objectives

Before reaching out to your network, determine your precise objectives and what you expect to accomplish via your contacts.

Having a defined objective will guide your activities and interactions.

Build Trust and Credibility
Establish trust and confidence within your network by delivering on commitments, being dependable, and retaining integrity.
Trust is the cornerstone of every effective network.

Prioritize Relationships
Focus on developing genuine, mutually beneficial connections within your network. - Quality relationships are frequently more important than numbers.

Understand Your Network's Strengths
Recognize the unique capabilities, knowledge, and resources of each relationship in your network.
Tailor your demands and partnerships depending on these strengths.

Offer Value First
Be proactive in giving aid, advice, or support to your contacts before asking their help.

Demonstrating your desire to give back builds your connections.

Be Clear and Respectful in Requests

When seeking help or cooperation, be brief, straightforward, and appreciative of your contacts' time.

Explain how the relationship might help your aims and why it's mutually beneficial.

Communicate Effectively

Maintain open and efficient contact with your network.

Keep connections updated about your progress, successes, and other pertinent changes.

Provide Regular Updates

Share updates about your initiatives, triumphs, and problems with your contacts.

Transparency fosters trust and keeps your network engaged.

Show Gratitude

Express thanks and appreciation to those who have helped you.

A simple thank-you may go a long way in establishing solid friendships.

Stay Connected Consistently

Keep in contact with your network periodically, even when you don't require urgent support.

Nurture connections throughout time to ensure they stay strong.

Be Open to Collaboration

Be open to collaborative possibilities within your network.

Partnerships and collaborative endeavors may lead to shared success.

Follow Through on Commitments

If you establish pledges or agreements with your relationships, ensure you follow through. - Reliability is vital for retaining confidence.

Leverage Technology and Platforms

Use social media, professional networking platforms, and internet tools to keep engaged and informed within your network.

Leveraging connections is a continual and dynamic activity that entails creating and maintaining relationships, identifying chances for cooperation, and being cognizant of the value you bring to others. When done correctly, utilizing your network may open doors, give support, and expedite your road toward success.

CHAPTER NINE

THE WEALTH CYCLE

Giving back refers to the act of contributing to the well-being of others or supporting causes that correspond with your ideals. It entails offering your resources, time, or experience with the community or groups in need.

Karma of Abundance: The notion of giving back is frequently related to the belief that what you put out into the world returns back to you. When you freely donate your resources, whether it's money, expertise, or time, it may generate a positive circle of plenty. People who follow this idea think that the act of giving might attract additional financial riches into their life.

Enhanced Reputation: Generosity and generosity may boost your personal or corporate image. A favorable reputation may lead to possibilities, relationships, and higher financial success. When people or corporations are renowned for their charitable activities, it may attract consumers, clients, and investors who wish to support socially responsible enterprises.

Networking and Connections: Engaging in charitable activities frequently entails contact with a wide set of individuals, including other contributors, volunteers, and recipients. These contacts may lead to significant connections and networking possibilities. Building a powerful network may open doors to financial possibilities, collaborations, and investments.

Tax Benefits: In many countries, charitable gifts come with tax advantages. When you contribute to charity organizations or causes, you may be entitled for tax deductions or credits. These financial incentives might lower your tax obligation, indirectly boosting your wealth.

The Joy of Philanthropy

The pleasure of generosity highlights the inherent benefits of giving. It's the profound pleasure and enjoyment that comes from having a good effect on others' lives or supporting causes that important to you.

Fulfillment and Well-Being: Research has shown that actions of charity and philanthropy may increase your feeling of contentment and general well-being. When you feel pleased and fulfilled, it may significantly improve your mental and emotional health. This, in turn, may boost your capacity to concentrate, make wise financial choices, and seek wealth-building possibilities.

Motivation to Succeed: Many people discover that the satisfaction they receive via giving acts as incentive to pursue financial success. Knowing that their financial fortune may be utilized to make a difference in the world drives people to work more, invest better, and build their wealth.

Long-Term Happiness: Philanthropy gives a source of long-lasting enjoyment. Unlike the transient pleasure of financial items, the feeling of purpose and satisfaction received from helping others may be maintained over time. This continuous happiness may significantly affect your thinking, resilience, and financial decision-making.

The Ripple Effect of Generosity

The ripple effect of giving is the belief that one act of kindness or generosity may cause a chain reaction, influencing not just the receiver but also others in the community. It demonstrates how little efforts may lead to large, far-reaching beneficial outcomes.

Positive Impact on Community: When you give to your community via acts of charity or philanthropy, you help build a more dynamic and successful environment. A vibrant community may, in turn, create a favorable climate for economic development and financial opportunity.

Enhanced Social Capital: Generosity frequently leads to enhanced social capital, which refers to the worth of your social networks and interactions. When you actively contribute in improving your community or supporting causes, you establish trust and goodwill. This social capital may be beneficial in both personal and corporate situations, possibly leading to financial gains.

Inspiration for Others: Your actions of charity may motivate others to do the same. As more people get interested in philanthropy and giving back, the aggregate influence may build a more supportive and successful society. This, in turn, may lead to economic development and possibilities that benefit everyone, including you.

Giving back, feeling the thrill of charity, and appreciating the ripple impact of kindness are all intertwined with financial riches. They not only provide the possibility for financial rewards but also contribute to personal well-being, motivation, and the construction of a more successful and integrated community. While the direct financial rewards of generosity may not always be immediate or quantifiable, they may be large and durable.

CONCLUSION

In the journey we've embarked upon throughout this book, we've studied the deep elements of obtaining financial freedom and enjoying a life of wealth and independence. We've gone into the key ideas that support this goal, from comprehending the route to financial freedom to unlocking the pleasure of charity and recognizing the ripple impact of generosity. As we close, let's reflect on the transforming power of these principles and how they intersect to produce a life of genuine prosperity.

Financial independence is not only about acquiring large quantities of money; it's about obtaining control over your finances and, by implication, your life. It's about having the liberty to make decisions that correspond with your beliefs, ambitions, and objectives. By grasping the fundamentals of financial independence, you've taken the first step toward opening the doors to a life where financial anxieties no longer influence your actions.

Financial freedom is the consequence of focused labor, intelligent financial decisions, and a clear picture of your objectives. It's about producing sources of passive income, reducing debt, and developing a sound financial foundation. Throughout this book, you've received insights into practical ways for reaching financial independence, and you've discovered that this route is both feasible and immensely satisfying.

True abundance surpasses mere prosperity. It includes a deep feeling of gratitude, satisfaction, and an appreciation for the richness of life beyond monetary metrics. You've realized that accepting abundance involves appreciating the importance of experiences, relationships, and personal development. It's an attitude that opens the way to greater satisfaction and enduring contentment.

Philanthropy is not reserved for the exceedingly affluent; it's a behavior that anybody can embrace. The pleasure of charity extends beyond the act of donating; it's about feeling the deep gratification of having a good effect on the lives of others. Through generosity, you've learned that money is not just about accumulation but also about the significant and permanent influence you can generate in the world.

The ripple effect of generosity indicates that even modest actions of compassion and giving may trigger a chain reaction of good change. By embracing generosity, you've become part of a bigger movement that uplifts communities, encourages others, and contributes to a more supportive and affluent society. This ripple effect spreads far beyond your personal circle, reaching individuals you may never know yet profoundly touch.

Gaining financial freedom, seeking financial independence, and enjoying a life of wealth are not alone efforts. They are interwoven components of a holistic approach to wealth. The ideas you've examined in this book are not merely theoretical notions; they are the building blocks of a more meaningful, purposeful, and successful life.

As you continue ahead on your path, remember that genuine wealth is not just defined by the size of your bank account but by the depth of your experiences, the richness of your relationships, and the positive effect you make on the world. Embrace these ideas with devotion and enthusiasm, and you will discover that financial prosperity and freedom are not destinations but lifetime companions on your way to a life well lived.

APPENDIX

Resources for Further Learning and Financial Tools

As you explore the realm of mastering wealth and financial success, this appendix presents a selection of essential resources, including suggested books and websites, as well as handy financial tools and applications to assist your journey:

1. Resources for Further Learning:
Online Courses: Platforms like Coursera, Udemy, and edX provide a broad choice of financial courses for in-depth study.

Local Workshops: Seek out local workshops and seminars on personal finance, investment, and wealth creation.

Financial Blogs: Follow credible financial blogs and websites like Investopedia, The Motley Fool, and NerdWallet for up-to-date information.

Podcasts: Tune in to financial podcasts such as "The Dave Ramsey Show," "Afford Anything," and "The Clark Howard Podcast" for professional guidance and inspiration.

Library: Visit your local library for a broad assortment of books, periodicals, and resources on personal finance and investing.

2. Recommended Books and Websites:
   Books:

   - "Rich Dad Poor Dad" by Robert Kiyosaki "The Millionaire Next Door" by Thomas J. Stanley and William D. Danko

   - "The Total Money Makeover" by Dave Ramsey

   - "Your Money or Your Life" by Vicki Robin and Joe Dominguez

Websites:

[Bogleheads](https://www.bogleheads.org/): A community of investors exchanging expertise on low-cost, passive investment.

[The Balance](https://www.thebalance.com/): Offers realistic guidance on personal finance, investment, and retirement planning.

[Mint](https://www.mint.com/): A popular budgeting and financial monitoring software with a multitude of educational materials.

3. Financial Tools and Apps:

- Mint: A complete budgeting and cost monitoring tool that delivers insights into your financial patterns.

- Personal Capital: Offers tools for budgeting, investment monitoring, and retirement planning.

- YNAB (You Need a Budget): A budgeting tool focused on giving every dollar a task, letting you take charge of your money.

- Acorns: A micro-investment app that rounds up your ordinary purchases and invests the spare change.

Investment Apps: Consider platforms like Robinhood, ETRADE, or Vanguard for managing your money.

These information and tools are excellent companions on your road toward financial mastery. Whether you're wanting to enhance your knowledge, obtain insights from professionals, or manage your money more efficiently, the information and tools in this appendix may help your quest of financial success.

[1]

---

[1] Positive Mindset for Wealth